This book is dedicated to Merrill and Pat Austin.
Our Hill Country sojourners, moon seekers, neighbors, and friends.

Contents

Introduction

This book is all about the many ways (there are actually a lot more than 50) of making your photos look better and sharing your masterpieces with others. Let's face it: If you want to make a photo that is too dark a little lighter, you don't want a five-page explanation about light theory. You just want to know what steps are necessary to do it. That's what this book is all about: how to do cool (and necessary) stuff using Elements 4.

Who Should Read This Book

Before digital photography became so popular, photography was all about taking rolls of film to a photo processor and hoping for the best. The digital camera has changed all of that. While you can still take your digital image to the same photo processor and accept what they give you, there is a better way. Using the power of Adobe Photoshop Elements 4, you can bring light into a darkened photo, make a flat, lifeless photo into one with vivid colors, and even perform photo magic—removing physical distractions like warts, blemishes and even a few extra pounds.

If you are new to Photoshop Elements or you have just dabbled with previous versions of the program but realize there is more you can do if you only knew how, this is the book for you. As an experienced photographer and graphics designer myself, I designed this book for those readers whose time is a precious commodity. The content from the previous edition has been rewritten and the material distilled into the topics that are most important to folks who want to make their photos look better, fix old or damaged photos, share them on the Web, or just print them out.

Who This Book Is Not For

If you recently won a Nobel Prize, this book isn't for you. This book does not teach you the theory of color, light, or the secrets of alchemy. Also, if you need a book that explains how each tool in Photoshop Elements 4 works in minute detail, I can offer a recommendation…it's called the user's manual. I have a copy myself and it comes with Photoshop Element 4. Although my book shows you a lot about Elements, it is not a 1,000+ page reference manual for the product that resembles a Manhattan phone directory.

Overview

The first two chapters are for those readers who just want the bare essentials. They contain the topics that you need to know to begin using Photoshop Elements right away. Chapter 1, "Introducing Photoshop Elements 4," is a brief introduction to Elements and what the program can do for you. The second chapter, "Just the Facts—The Basics of Using Elements," covers basic stuff, such as the layout of the program, tool names, and how to do a few simple things like getting your photos into your computer, automatically fixing photos, and attaching your photo wonders to an e-mail.

Since the most common problems faced by photographers has to do with lighting or color, Chapters 3 and 4 shows you how to use Elements not only to correct common lighting problems but also to control the color in your photographs, allowing your colors to be both correct and vivid. These chapters also show how you can correct a myriad of other common photo problems, including the all-important topics of improving image composition (both size and content), as well as adjusting and enhancing your photos.

With all of the digital photos that have accumulated and will continue to accumulate in your computer, you will need to know how to organize them. Chapter 5 is all about organizing your photo collection. You will discover how to make the most of the powerful Organizer built into Elements 4. This naturally flows into the two chapters that follow: Chapters 6 and 7.

The first half of the book mostly focuses on making your photos look good. Chapters 6 and 7 are about all the fun things that you can do with Elements whether it's moving people from one photo to another or replacing an overcast sky. Chapter 6, "Dazzling Effects and Professional Techniques," is a big chapter packed with many step-by-step projects. Chapter 7, "Fun with Type, Shapes, and Cookie Cutter Tools," explains some of the effects that are possible with Photoshop Elements. This chapter teaches you how to add titles to photos for a more professional look, how to add cartoon-like thought balloons to pictures, and shows you how you can turn photos into different shapes.

I refer to the next two chapters as the photographic repair shop and it covers two important topics: retouching and repairing photographs. In Chapter 8, "Retouching Photos Like a Pro," you'll learn how easy it is to remove braces on teeth and brighten eyes with the stroke of a Brush tool. You'll also learn how to reshape body parts to compensate for bad camera angles during shooting. Chapter 9, "Scanning and Repairing Photographs," is an important chapter in which you discover how to salvage photographs that you might have thought were beyond repair.

Making panoramas is one of my favorite subjects so I spend way too many pages showing you how to photograph and then use the PhotoMerge command in Elements to make stunning panoramas.

The last chapter is all about sharing photos. Whether you are printing the photos and mailing them or creating a slide show and burning it onto a CD, this chapter shows you how easy it is to make photo creations that are super easy and yet look very professional.

Step-by-Step Tutorials

As someone who has sat in more than his fair share of photo-editing classes, I know that anything I learn by watching someone else do, that it doesn't stick. If I actually do the procedure or technique being described, I have a much better chance of recalling it later when I need to use it. This book contains a lot of step-by-step tutorials. To let you work along with those tutorials, the sample files are available for download at **www.peachpit.com/50coolwaysPSE4.**

Acknowledgments

This is the part of the book that reads like a speech by an Oscar winner. Let's face it, when you see your favorite actor or actress on the silver screen, you don't see the hundreds of people that are needed to make the movie. Now that movie credits include everyone involved in a production, you get a better idea of just what it takes to create a movie. This book represents the combined efforts of a large cast of hard-working craftspeople and artists. If I listed everyone who made a contribution to this edition, it would take up a large number of pages. So like a winning speech at the Academy Awards with a three-minute time limit, here are the people (coworkers and friends) that I want to recognize for their efforts.

First of all, I want to thank the crew on the Adobe Photoshop Elements development team who worked long and hard to create this version of Elements. Special thanks to Adobe's Mark Dahm and Richard Coencas who patiently listened to my ranting and raving during the early stages of the product development.

Several folk at Peachpit Press really had to go above and beyond to get this book into your hands. I want to thank my editor, Karyn Johnson, who put in some long, long hours to get all of the parts of the book together. I also want to thank our hard-working copy editor, Emilia Thiuri, as well as Becky Winter and Kate Kaminski, for their expertise in production and layout. My technical editor, David Plotkin, agreed to go through the manuscript to ensure that all of the content and tutorials work the way they are supposed to.

I especially want to thank all of the people that let me use their pictures in the book, especially Cooper Morin. I must also include thanks to my family who puts up with my long absences while I work on writing books. Well, my time is up, and my final thank you is to all of those who buy these books because without you, all of this effort would be for naught.

1 Introducing Photoshop Elements 4

If this is the first time you've used Photoshop Elements, let me tell you a little about what you can expect from this program. A few years ago, Adobe realized that a growing number of consumers were demanding professional-level photo-editing tools, but did not want or need many of the features in Photoshop, the industry standard for photo editing. As digital cameras have improved every year, so has the need for better tools to manipulate and output the resulting photographs. Photoshop Elements specifically addresses the needs of photographers, especially digital photographers.

What is Photoshop Elements?

In short, Photoshop Elements is a powerful image editor that will meet many of your digital photography needs. You can use Elements to do the following, and more:

- Import images from your digital camera (or card reader) into your computer.

- Crop, enhance, and color correct your photos.

- Manipulate your photos. It is a universal law of photography that the best-looking photo of you is coupled with either someone you are no longer attached to, or the worst possible picture of a loved one. Elements can change all that with the sweep of a mouse.

- Organize your photos. If you own a digital camera, the hard drive on your computer will soon be overflowing with photos scattered throughout many different folders. You need a photographic memory or an image manager to keep track of your personal photo gallery. The Organizer in Elements will do all of that and more.

- Share your photos with everyone you know. Whether you want to print your photos and mail them, email your photos, or make an electronic slide show, Elements gives you the ability to do it quickly and more importantly, do it automatically.

What's the Difference between Photoshop and Photoshop Elements 4?

This is one of the most asked questions I encounter. It is easy to think of Elements as a stripped-down version of Photoshop because the two programs look and act in a similar fashion. The first time I met the product manager for Elements I think I referred to it as a "crippled version" of Photoshop. I couldn't have been further from the truth. I think of Elements as Photoshop repurposed for the digital photographer. Elements offers most of the professional-level tools found in the more expensive Photoshop. The major difference between Elements and its more famous cousin is that Elements focuses on simplifying the process of digital photo editing. Are there features in Photoshop CS2 that I wish were in Elements? Sure there are. Are those additional tools worth the extra dollars? Not for a majority of users.

What's New in Version 4?

This question is very popular among owners of previous versions of Elements. It's generally asked because current owners are wondering if there are enough new goodies to justify paying for the upgrade. The most substantial change (the one that has drawn the greatest attention in the media anyway) is that for the first time only the PC version has been upgraded; the Mac version remains unchanged at version 3. This fact does not mean Adobe doesn't like the Mac—it was, simply, a business decision not to update the Mac version at this time. Here is a brief summary of features and tools that either are new or have been improved upon in Photoshop Elements 4.

What's New in Editor?

The workspace area of Elements where you can make edits to your images is called the Editor. There are a few new features in the Editor worth mentioning.

Adjust Color for Skin Tone

This new tool is quite easily the best way to correct color in a photo and is one of my favorites. Click an area of skin and watch the tonal balance of all colors in the photo improve (**Figure 1.1**).

Figure 1.1
The Adjust Color for Skin Tone tool quickly and accurately corrects colors in a photo.

Two New Magic Tools

The Magic Selection Brush and the Magic Extractor tools are both new in Elements 4. Making selections can be time-consuming, which is why these tools are so useful. With them, you can automatically select portions of your photos or simply select an object in a photo and extract it from its background (**Figure 1.2**).

Figure 1.2
The Magic Extractor tool quickly removes backgrounds from photos so that they can be replaced.

Red Eye Removal

The Red Eye Removal tool is totally automatic and you can even set it to automatically detect and remove red eye from photos as they are being imported (**Figure 1.3**).

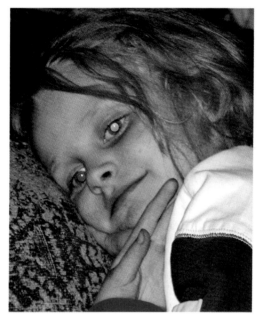 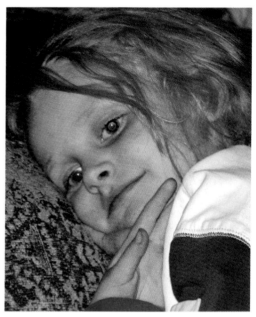

Figure 1.3
Red eye removal has been improved even more.

Straighten Tool

Another great new tool allows you to straighten a photo (like the one taken from a moving car as shown in **Figure 1.4**) by dragging a horizontal or vertical line across an image and then adjusting the image along that horizontal or vertical plane.

Figure 1.4
The Straighten tool provides an easy way to straighten photos in a flash.

What's New or Improved in Organizer?

You use the Organizer to find, organize, and share your media files. This is where you'll go to create tags, assign categories, develop slide shows, and order prints.

Face Tagging

With this new tool, you can select a group of photos, and then Photoshop Elements isolates and displays all the faces in the photos so that you can apply tags to them (**Figure 1.5**).

Figure 1.5
Face tagging is a fast way to find and tag any face in a photo.

Search by Metadata

Now you can search for a variety of metadata criteria, such as filename, file type, shutter speed, camera model, date, and tags. You can even perform a search on multiple criteria.

Improved Multimedia Slide Show

The ability to create a cool slide show has been greatly improved (**Figure 1.6**). When moving between slides there are now over 50 professional slide transitions to wow your viewers. You can add text to any slide by the click of a button and you can also add graphics to add something extra. Instead of viewing a single slide you can now pan and zoom across a slide. This means you can begin with a small part of a slide—such as showing the face of a child—and then zoom out to reveal the rest of the image. Once the visual is complete, you can add music to the slide show using either the music selections provided by Adobe or your own favorites. The editing tools allow you to quickly change the order of the slides and change the timing so it fits the length of the selected music.

Figure 1.6
Now you can make professional-quality slide shows with even more cool effects and features.

Improved Photo Mail

Instead of attaching photos to emails, with Photo Mail you can turn a boring email into a theme-based Photo Mail with layouts, frames, and captions (**Figure 1.7**).

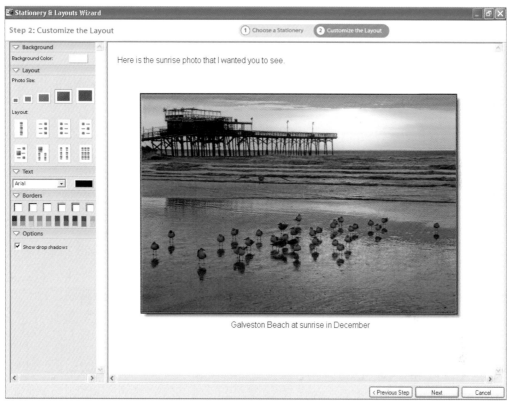

Figure 1.7
Instead of attaching files to an email, send your photos to friends and loved ones as Photo Mail.

Hardware Requirements for Elements 4

As Elements continues to improve, the minimum hardware and operating system requirements change as well. The following hardware requirements are the minimum needed to operate the system:

- Intel® Pentium® III, 4, or 5 processor, 800 MHz

- Windows XP with SP2, Home Media Center

- 256 MB of RAM

- 600 MB of available hard-disk space

- A monitor resolution of 1024 by 768 pixels or greater

- Internet Explorer 5.0, 5.5, or 6.0 (updated with applicable Service Packs)

- CD-ROM drive

To this list I would make the following recommendations in order of importance:

- 512 MB RAM instead of 256 MB

- CD or DVD recorder (burner)

Speeding Elements Up

As with all graphics programs, there are some computer upgrades that will make your software run faster and others that will have little to no effect. Here are a few suggestions:

- Adding more RAM to your computer is the best choice to improve performance. If you have less than 512 MB you will probably see an improvement by adding additional RAM. Check with your computer manufacturer to see what options are available to you for additional RAM.

- Adding a high-performance graphics card will not improve the performance of Elements. These cards are designed to improve video game performance and offer little to no noticeable improvement to digital photo editing.

- Although Adobe lists Intel processors in the minimum requirements, Elements will also work on a Windows machine using an AMD processor.

Now you know a little bit about Elements and what is necessary to run it. In the next chapter, we'll cover the basic stuff you need to know to do the projects described in the remainder of this book. Although it may seem there are way too many palettes, tools, and other items to recall, remember that you can get great results from this program by using only a few of the important ones.

2

Just the Facts—The Basics of Using Photoshop Elements

This is a chapter for those in a hurry. It is a no-frills chapter about how to do the most common tasks using Photoshop Elements. It takes you from downloading the photo to sharing the photo with others.

Navigating in the Workspaces

Because Elements is actually two programs it has two main workspaces: the Editor and the Organizer. The Editor (**Figure 2.1a**) is where you fix and manipulate your photos, while the Organizer (**Figure 2.1b**) is where you organize and make cool creations to share with friends.

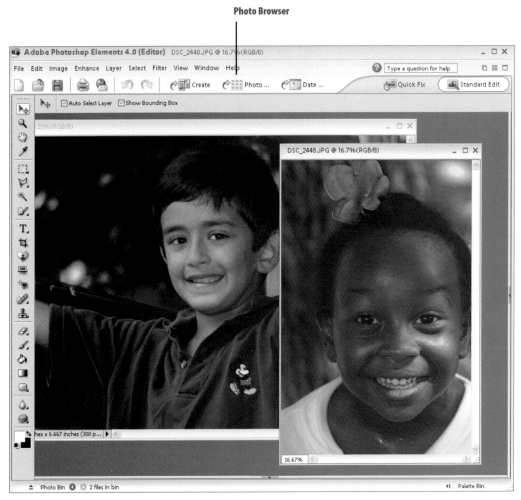

Figure 2.1a
The Editor is where you fix and manipulate your photos.

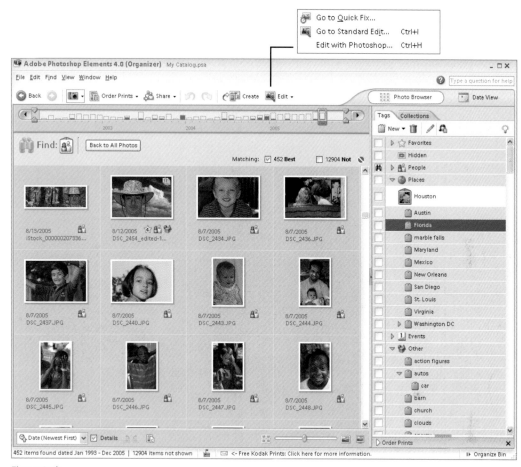

Figure 2.1b
The Organizer is where you find, organize, and share your photos.

Opening Elements—So Many Choices

When you launch Photoshop Elements a Welcome screen appears (**Figure 2.2**, next page), presenting you with several choices to make. As you drag the cursor over each button, the welcome screen changes to show a brief description of that particular option. Here is a brief summary of the choices:

- **Product Overview.** A multi-page, high-level overview of Elements.

- **View and Organize Photos.** Launches the Organizer.

- **Quickly Fix Photos.** Launches the Editor in Quick Fix mode.

- **Edit and Enhance Photos.** Launches the Editor in Standard Edit mode.

- **Make Photo Creations.** Launches the Organizer and opens the Creations menu.

- **Start From Scratch.** Launches the Editor with New File open.

- **Tutorials.** Connects to Adobe tutorials using the Internet.

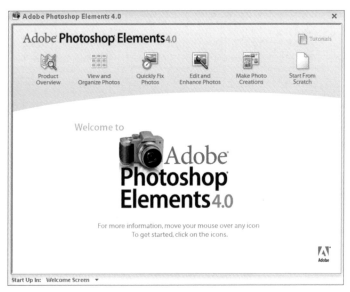

Figure 2.2
The Welcome screen offers several choices when Elements is launched.

The Elements Editor

The Editor has two modes of operation: Standard Edit and Quick Fix.

Standard Edit Mode

This is the traditional editor workspace (**Figure 2.3**), which is familiar to Photoshop Elements users. From this workspace you can do just about anything to your images, including correcting color problems, creating special effects, or generally improving the photos.

Select Quick Fix.

Select Standard Edit.

Figure 2.3
The Standard Edit mode offers two modes of operation.

Quick Fix Mode

When the Quick Fix button in Standard Edit is clicked, the screen is filled with a work-space optimized to quickly fix an image with the most commonly used controls on the screen and a real-time selectable preview display (**Figure 2.4**, next page). If you are new to digital imaging, Quick Fix is a good place to start fixing photos. It has many automatic tools for correcting color and lighting.

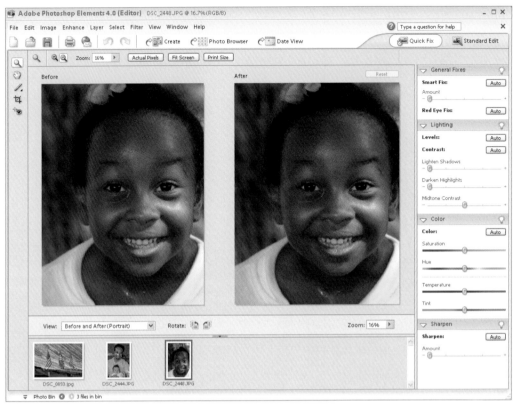

Figure 2.4
The Quick Fix mode offers all the controls needed to quickly enhance a photo.

The Organizer

Use the Organizer to find, organize, and share your photos and media files. Like the Editor, the Organizer also has two modes of operation: Photo Browser and Date View.

Photo Browser

This is an image management application that helps you organize your photo collection and it provides a visual display of the photos in the catalog (**Figure 2.5**). The Photo Browser lists all the photos and any other cataloged assets in a single window that you can easily browse. You can view a single photo or thumbnails of all photos, depending on the size of thumbnail you specify from the thumbnail slider. It can even show thumbnail previews of images that are stored remotely, such as on CD or DVD.

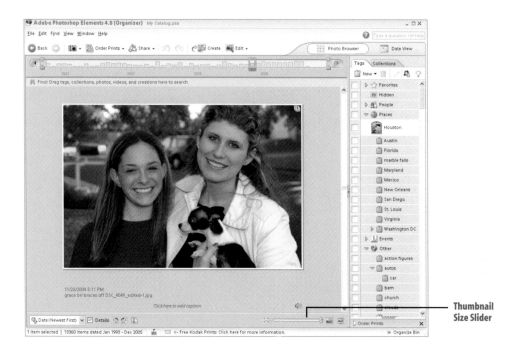

Thumbnail Size Slider

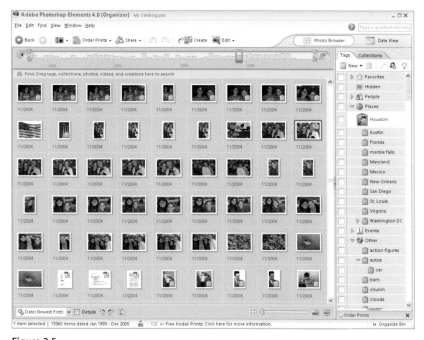

Figure 2.5
The Thumbnail Size Slider lets you quickly make the thumbnails the size that suits your needs.

Date View

The Date View offers a unique method of viewing photos in a calendar-style format (**Figure 2.6**).

Figure 2.6
In the Date View, you can display your images and sort them by date.

Now that you know the basic parts of the application, let's see how it works.

The Basic Steps to Using Elements

The quickest way to get pictures from your camera and ready for printing involves only three steps:

1. Move the photos from the camera to the computer.

2. Correct or enhance the photo.

3. Save and share the photo.

Connecting Camera and Computer

You need a way to get your pictures from the camera into the computer. To do this, you need a connection between the camera and the computer using one of the following connection types:

- A dedicated card reader

- A physical connection to the camera (called tethering)

The type of connection used determines how long it will take to move pictures from your camera to your computer. Card readers (**Figure 2.7**) are faster than almost any other connection and are very inexpensive.

Figure 2.7
A card reader is one of the fastest ways to download your photos.

Whichever connection you use, when you attach the reader or camera to the computer, the operating system detects it and presents you with some choices.

TIP

A computer treats a digital camera and a card reader the same.

Connecting to a Computer

When you attach a camera or card reader to a computer, the operating system detects it and opens a list (**Figure 2.8**) asking you to select the action you want to take.

Figure 2.8
Windows asks you what action to take after you've plugged in a camera or card reader.

Regardless of any action you may or may not take, in a few moments the Photo Downloader opens (often over the Windows list—**Figure 2.9**).

Transferring Photos

Transferring the photos is simple. Here is how it is done:

1. Select the source. The camera or card reader that you just connected should already appear in the Get Photos from pull-down menu.

2. Choose a place to save the files. There are several options here. The default location for photos is My Documents\My Pictures\Adobe\Digital Camera Photos. Pay close attention to the Create Subfolder Using option. If this option is checked, each time you copy photos into Elements the pictures will load into separate folders labeled by a date/time stamp or a name you assign to them. The Date/Time of Import option creates a stamp name that is long and complicated, so if you do use the subfolder option you may want to consider assigning your own name.

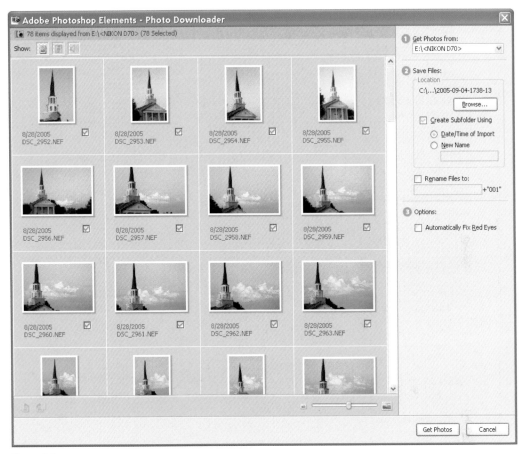

Figure 2.9
The Photo Downloader automates the transfer of your photos into your computer.

3. Automatically Fix Red Eyes. This is a new feature in Elements 4. If this option is checked, Elements will process each photo looking for red eye. If you don't have photos with red eye it's a real time-waster to use this.

4. Select the photos you want to download into your computer by clicking the check marks next to the thumbnails of your photos. In most cases you want all of them but if not, simply uncheck the photos you don't want. Similar to the way the Photo Browser works, you can control the size of the thumbnails in the Photo Downloader with the slider at the bottom of the screen.

5. Transfer the photos. Click the Get Photos button to begin the transfer (**Figure 2.10**).

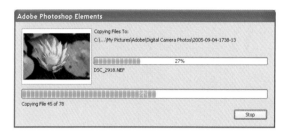

Figure 2.10
This dialog shows the progress of the image transfer.

6. After the transfer is complete, the Photo Browser displays the photos just imported. If the photos you download are already in Organizer you will get a list of the photos that were not imported (**Figure 2.11**).

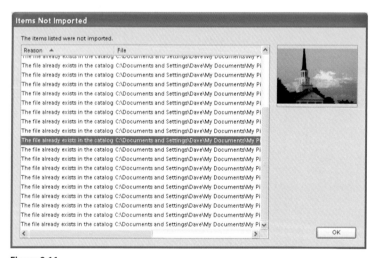

Figure 2.11
When the transfer is complete, one of these two dialogs appears.

The last thing Photo Downloader will ask is if you want to delete the photos on the camera memory card (**Figure 2.12**). This is up to you, but I recommend getting into the habit of first making sure the photos have transferred without any problems, and then clearing the memory card using the camera's delete feature.

TIP

If you know the Photo Browser catalog that you want to put the photos into, you can select the catalog before starting the transfer by clicking the Advanced Options button.

Figure 2.12
Elements gives you the choice to erase the image from the media card.

Opening the Photos

Once the photos are in your computer, there are several ways to get into Photoshop Elements to work on them:

- **From the Photo Browser.** Select the photo you want, and then either use the shortcut Ctrl+I, click the Standard Edit button, or choose Edit, Go to Standard Edit (**Figure 2.13**).

- **From the Menu bar in Editor.** Choose File, Open, and then locate the image or images you want.

Go to Standard Edit.   **Selected image**

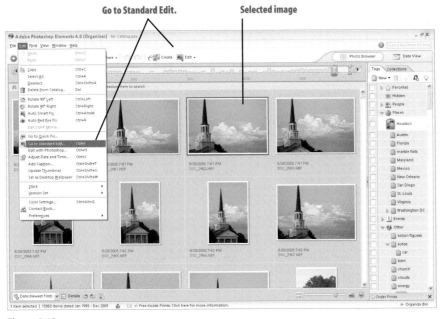

Figure 2.13
There are several ways to move photos from the Photo Browser to the Editor.

If you open an image for editing from the Photo Browser, the Editor launches (if it isn't already open) with the image in it. The thumbnail in the Photo Browser displays an icon that indicates that the image is being edited (**Figure 2.14**).

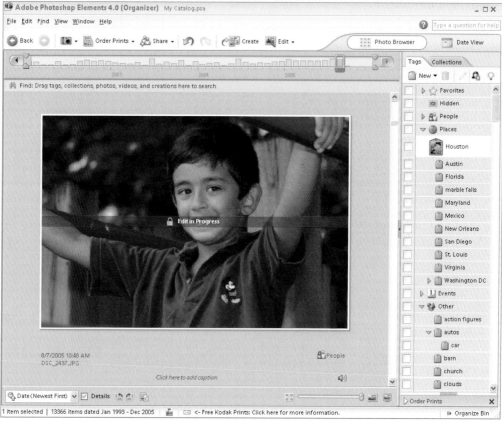

Figure 2.14
When a photo is being edited, an icon with the words "Edit in Progress" appears in the Photo Browser.

Rotating the Photos

This is the first and most common correction you'll make with Elements. Anytime you take a photograph with the camera in portrait orientation, it needs to be rotated. For the record, when we talk about the orientation of the camera, we are referring to what part of the image is on top—the wide part or the narrow part. **Figure 2.15** shows the same subject taken using two orientations: landscape and portrait.

With Photoshop Elements, there are many ways you can rotate a picture. For example, you can

- Use the Left and Right buttons in Photo Browser
- Use the Left and Right buttons in Full Screen Mode (Organizer)
- Use the Rotate command in Editor.

Figure 2.15
The left photo is taken in landscape orientation; the right photo is taken in portrait orientation.

Rotating Images with Photo Browser

Rotating a photo by using the Photo Browser is the simplest and quickest way. Simply select the thumbnails of the photos you need to rotate, and then click the button for the desired rotation direction at the bottom of the Photo Browser (**Figure 2.16**).

The Rotate Command—One Photo at a Time

It isn't necessary to use the Photo Browser to rotate images. You can also choose the Rotate from the Image menu in Editor and select the rotation that turns your photo right side up. Alternatively, you can right-click the thumbnail in the Photo Bin and choose left or right rotation (**Figure 2.17**)

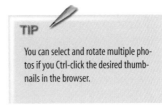

TIP

You can select and rotate multiple photos if you Ctrl-click the desired thumbnails in the browser.

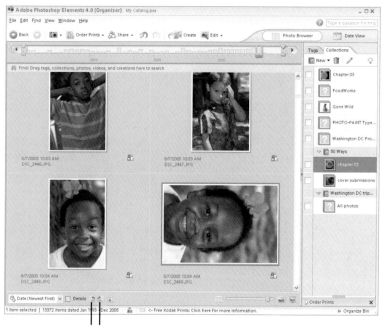

Rotate left Rotate right

Figure 2.16
The icons at the bottom of the Photo Browser provide a fast and easy way to rotate your photos to the correct orientation.

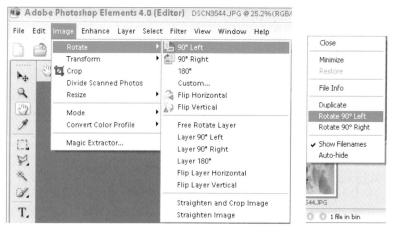

Figure 2.17
You can also rotate images from the Image menu in Editor (left) or by right-clicking a thumbnail (right).

Cropping

Now that your photos are all pointed the right way, the next step is to crop them (**Figure 2.18**). Generally, people don't think about cropping their photos because they feel they must keep every part of the photo. The truth is that most photographs are greatly improved by removing the part of the scene that distracts the viewer's eye. You can crop photos using the Crop tool (C) ⬚. Its operation is pretty obvious. The part that requires judgment on your part is what to crop and what to leave in the photo.

Using the Crop tool is simple. After you select the Crop tool, drag it over the part of the image that you want to keep. When you release the mouse button, the crop marquee appears as a bounding box with handles at the corners and sides. You can use these to adjust the crop marquee. When the photo is cropped the way you want it, click the Commit check mark floating in the lower-right corner (or you can just double-click the image). It crops according to your specifications.

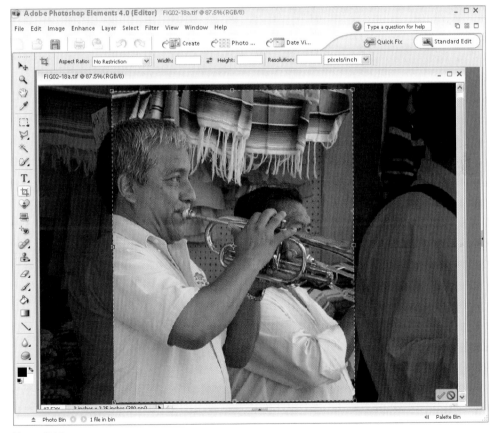

Figure 2.18
The Crop tool is simple to use.

What to Crop

This chapter only covers the basics, so consider these general rules when you decide what to remove from your photos:

- Decide what the subject of the photo is and remove anything that distracts from the subject.

- Avoid placing the subject in the center of the photo. This is called the rule of thirds and it is covered in more detail in Chapter 4, "Making Your Photos Look Professional."

Here is an example of the aforementioned points. The photo of the trumpet player in **Figure 2.19** has another man's shoulder in it and a fluorescent-colored price tag above the trumpeter's head. By cropping the photo to what's shown in **Figure 2.20**, the shoulder and price tag are gone and the trumpet player becomes the focus of the photo. The cropping also changed the orientation of the photo from landscape to portrait.

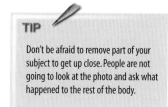

TIP

Don't be afraid to remove part of your subject to get up close. People are not going to look at the photo and ask what happened to the rest of the body.

Figure 2.19
This image needs some cropping to focus the attention on the subject.

Figure 2.20
Cropping improves the composition of this photo.

Enhancing Your Photos

I wish that you could just click a single button in Elements that automatically makes your picture perfect. The reason this button doesn't exist is because the computer doesn't have any way of knowing what's right and what's wrong with your photo. While that single button doesn't yet exist, Elements provides several different automatic tools that can improve your photos.

Auto Smart Fix: One-Stop Image Correction

Auto Smart Fix applies many different types of adjustments with a single action. It is located in the Enhance menu. Unlike Quick Fix, which has several interactive adjustment sliders, Auto Smart Fix is completely automatic—which is both good and bad.

Applying Auto Smart Fix to a photo can instantly make the photo look better. **Figure 2.21** is an example of Auto Smart Fix working perfectly. The original photo (photo on the top) was slightly overexposed and had a bluish color cast to it. As you can see in the photo on the bottom, Auto Smart Fix made the image appear more vibrant.

Figure 2.21
When Auto Smart Fix works, it works great.

The fully automatic approach doesn't always work. Sometimes it makes the photo worse. Since it is completely automatic, there are no options. If the Auto Smart Fix doesn't improve the photo, you need to Undo (Ctrl+Z) and use a different tool. An example is shown in **Figure 2.22**, which has a bluish color cast caused by the camera flash. Application of Auto Smart Fix makes the blue color cast even more blue (**Figure 2.23**).

Figure 2.22
The original photo has a slight, blue color cast caused by a flash.

Figure 2.23
Here is an example of when Auto Smart Fix adjusts the image and the result is not very good.

There is no way to tell in advance what types of images will be improved by Auto Smart Fix and which ones won't. I estimate that about seven out of ten are visibly improved. The images that contain dark backgrounds or were taken using a flash typically aren't good candidates.

If your image isn't improved using Auto Smart Fix, there are many other ways and tools to fix it, which are discussed in the next chapter. For example, using the new Adjust Color for Skin Tone tool does the job (**Figure 2.24**).

Figure 2.24
Adjust Color for Skin Tone does a better job.

Sorting Out the Good from the Bad

Some images cannot be salvaged. Either they are all black, all white, or most commonly, the auto-focus on your camera got faked out and the photo is a complete blur. I recommend that you make a habit of deleting these photos. If you don't, the number of these images grows at an alarming rate. Like all things in Elements there are several ways to delete photos. Here is an easy one that removes the photo from the Photo Browser and deletes it entirely:

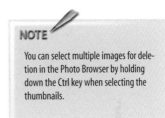

NOTE

You can select multiple images for deletion in the Photo Browser by holding down the Ctrl key when selecting the thumbnails.

1. Select the thumbnail of the photo you want to delete in the Photo Browser.

2. Press the Delete key. A warning message appears to make sure you want to delete the photo (**Figure 2.25**). Click Yes. The photo is removed from the catalog. If you click the check box as well, the image is moved to the Recycle Bin.

Figure 2.25
This warning appears when you attempt to delete an image.

Sharing Your Photos

According to most industry studies, the most common method of sharing photos is by email. The problem most people have is that the photos produced by their digital camera are so large, they gag their email service provider. So to send photos by email, they must be resized. The cool part is Elements will do it all for you. Here is how to share your photos via email:

1. From the Photo Browser, select the photo you want to send to someone, click the Share button, and choose E-mail (**Figure 2.26**). This opens the Attach Selected Items to E-mail dialog (**Figure 2.27**). Here you can add additional photos by clicking the Add button.

2. Add the name and email address of the recipient by selecting the names that appear in the Select Recipients list.

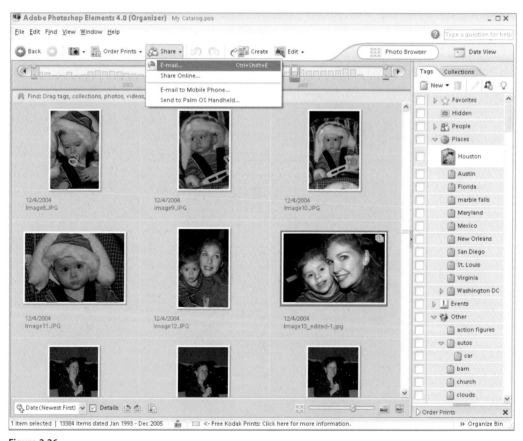

Figure 2.26
Sharing email is easy from Photo Browser.

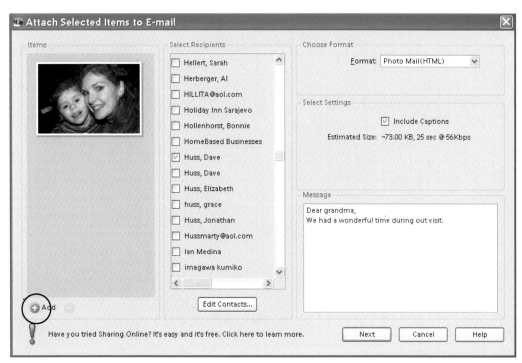

Figure 2.27
Pick the recipient and add your message.

3. Selecting Format, Photo Mail (HTML) in the Choose Format section works with most systems. If your recipients tell you that they can't open or see your photos, however, then I recommend you choose Individual Attachments.

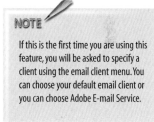

NOTE

If this is the first time you are using this feature, you will be asked to specify a client using the email client menu. You can choose your default email client or you can choose Adobe E-mail Service.

4. Now is the fun part. Click Next and then click the Stationary & Layouts button. This opens a wizard-style selection that takes you step by step through the options of creating a really cool email (**Figure 2.28**, next page). When you finish, you are returned to the Attach Selected Items to E-mail dialog, where you can add a message to the email.

5. In the Customize the Layout page (**Figure 2.29**, next page) you can change the photo size. If you have more than one photo you can change the layout for each one and decide how the photos will appear in the email.

6. Clicking Next Step launches your default email service and the email appears, ready to send. At this time, you can add additional email recipients from your email address book. Click the Send button, and you have created a really cool email (**Figure 2.30**, page 33).

Figure 2.28
Choose the stationery to enhance your photo.

Figure 2.29
Change the size and layout.

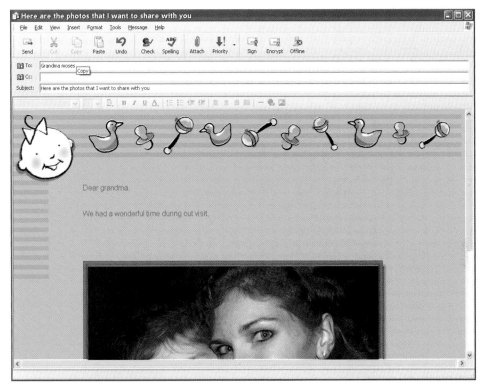

Figure 2.30
Completed Photo Mail.

Now you know how to do the quick and slick stuff with Elements. In the next chapter we will learn some more of the tools and how to go beyond the basics. You will discover some new automatic tools and learn how to fix those photos that couldn't be enhanced with the Auto Smart Fix.

3 Making Photos Look Their Best

Now that digital cameras are being used by most consumers, you can go to your favorite photo developer, plug your camera memory card into a kiosk, select your favorite shots, and—presto!—you have photographs. Although I can understand the appeal of popping in the media and receiving prints, I always want to fiddle with my photos a little (sometimes a lot) before I show them around. In this chapter, we'll discover how easy it is to make your photos look better before you share them, whether it is by email or by printing them.

There are only a few steps that are involved in making your photos look great, and while the steps are listed in their recommended order, it is not necessary to do them all—or any of them. After all, some pictures look perfect right out of the camera.

So, we'll begin with the first step—improving the composition.

Better Photos Through Cropping

Chapter 2 introduced the Crop tool and basic techniques for creating a good crop. Now that you know what it is, let's examine this important topic in more detail.

There are basically two reasons to crop a photo: To improve the composition of the subject in the photo and to change the aspect ratio to fit a standard photo size, if you plan to make prints of the photos. We'll begin by looking at how to crop for composition.

Cropping Controls What the Viewer Sees

To demonstrate how important cropping is in creating the overall visual impact of a photo, look at the original photo in **Figure 3.1**. I took this photo when our friends celebrated their 25th wedding anniversary and renewed their wedding vows—with their nine children in attendance.

If I do a tight crop as shown in **Figure 3.2**, the real subject becomes the young man who is embarrassed by the sight of mom and dad smooching.

Figure 3.1
A typical wedding photo, right?

Figure 3.2
Cropping changes the whole mood and subject of the photo.

Simple Rules of Composition

The rules for good composition apply to both taking the original photo and cropping it. You should either try to fill the frame with the subject (**Figure 3.3**), or follow the "rule of thirds" (see the sidebar, "The Rule of Thirds").

Figure 3.3
Cropping the photo to fill the frame is an effective solution.

The advantage of filling the frame with your subject is that it's simple to do. Here is how it is done:

1. Select the Crop tool—(C) or .

2. Click and drag the tool over the area to be selected. The area to be removed appears dark (**Figure 3.4**).

3. Adjust the handles to fine-tune the area to be cropped. You can move the entire crop selection marquee around the image by clicking inside the crop selection and dragging it to a new position.

4. When the composition looks right, either double-click inside the cropped area or click the Commit check mark in the lower part of the image.

The Rule of Thirds

With the rule of thirds, you mentally divide the crop area with two evenly spaced vertical lines and two evenly spaced horizontal lines, creating a grid of nine sections. To create a pleasing composition, the primary focal point of the image should fall at one of the line intersections. Avoid placing the focal point in the dead center of the image, as this generally creates a bland composition.

Figure 3.4
Click and drag the tool over the area to be selected.

Making Photos Fit to Print

Most digital cameras create pictures with different ratios of height to width (called an aspect ratio) than traditional 35-mm film cameras. This difference determines what will and will not appear in a printed photo.

The dimensions of standard 35-mm film are 36 by 24 mm, which translates into an aspect ratio of 3:2. In contrast, typical digital camera sensors have an aspect ratio of 4:3. This means that your digital camera pictures are slightly taller or wider than those you take with your film camera. This affects what eventually ends up in your prints, and

NOTE

If the photos are only to be shared electronically, aspect ratios do not affect the viewing.

you should keep it in mind when cropping photos for printing. The loss isn't a lot, but this small loss can ruin a photo if the subject matter goes from edge to edge. Always try to leave a little space between the subject and the edge of your photos when taking your pictures to compensate for any edge loss when printing using standard photo sizes.

How to Crop to a Print Size

The aspect ratio of all 35-mm film is 3:2 and the aspect ratio of standard photo sizes is different for each size. **Figures 3.5–3.8** shows what is lost from a digital photo when printed using a few popular photo sizes.

Figure 3.5
Original Photo of the U.S. Supreme Court during the Cherry Blossom Festival.

Figure 3.6
Photo cropped as
a 4 x 6-inch print.

Lost portion of photo

Figure 3.7
Photo cropped as
a 5 x 7-inch print.

Lost portion of photo

Supreme Court.jpg @ 50%(RGB/8*)

50.05% | 4 inches x 2.999 inches (355.75 ppi)

Lost portion of photo

Figure 3.8
Same photo cropped
as an 8 x 10-inch
print.

If you know that the photo is going to be printed, you can set the Crop tool to the correct dimensions so the photo can be cropped to the correct aspect ratio. Here is how it is done:

1. Open a photo and select the Crop tool (C).

2. In the Crop Tool Options bar, select 4 x 6 in from the Aspect Ratio pull-down menu (**Figure 3.9**, next page).

3. Click and drag the Crop tool into the image. The aspect ratio of the tool is locked at the preset you selected. In my example (**Figure 3.10**, next page), I cropped out the lower portion of the columns.

4. When you have the image cropped the way you like it, click the Commit check mark at the bottom right of the image. Your photo is ready to be printed as a 4 x 6 without unexpected loss of material at the edges.

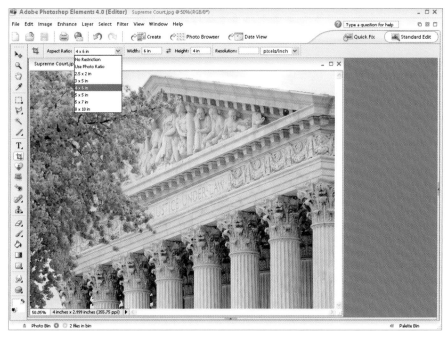

Figure 3.9
Select a standard photo size.

Click here to complete
the crop.

Figure 3.10
Clicking Commit completes the cropping action.

Fast Facts About Cropping

Here are some quick facts and tips about using the Crop tool that you should know about.

- When you're finished using a preset crop setting, make it a habit to clear the Aspect Ratio setting by changing it to No Restriction in the Crop Tool Options bar. If you don't, the next time you use the Crop tool to make a freehand crop, you'll wonder why it doesn't work correctly.

- To flip the width and the height settings in the Options bar, click the Swap Height and Width icon.

- Pressing the Escape key clears the selected cropping area.

- You can move the marquee to another position in the image by placing the pointer inside the bounding box and dragging.

- You can change both the color and opacity of the crop shield (the cropped area surrounding the image) by changing the Crop tool preferences. Choose Edit, Preferences, Display & Cursors and specify a new Color and Opacity value in the Crop Tool area of the Preferences dialog (**Figure 3.11**). If you don't want to see a colored shield while cropping, deselect Use Shield.

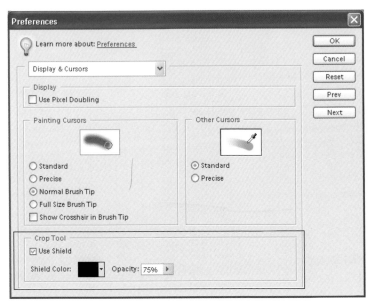

Figure 3.11
The Crop Tool preferences can be adjusted for the photo you are working on.

Cropping Versus Picture Size

If you watch TV or go to the movies, you have probably seen a critical scene where someone asks a technician to zoom in on some part of a video or satellite photo, at which point, my favorite line is said: "Now enhance it." Amazingly, the blurred license plate or face or whatever suddenly comes into crystal-clear focus. Don't believe it—it only happens in the movies. The point is, when you crop away a large part of a photo to create the composition you want, be careful that you haven't reduced your photo to the size of a postage stamp. There are times when you must crop out a large percentage of a photo to get the composition that you want. At times like this, having a camera with a large sensor (4 or more megapixels) comes in handy.

If you want only to show the picture on the Web, the image size can be relatively small. If, on the other hand, you want to print a photo, you need to have enough remaining size to print the image at a resolution of 150 dots-per-inch (dpi) to get a crisp and clean photo.

Straighten the Picture

A common problem with photos is that they are crooked. The subject matter often determines if the uneven condition is noticeable or not. Generally speaking, close-up nature photos (**Figure 3.12**) lack a horizontal reference and don't appear crooked.

Figure 3.12
A nature photo rarely appears crooked.

Is the photo in **Figure 3.13** crooked? There is no horizontal reference and any viewer looking a gas prices that low would not notice if it was crooked or not.

Straightening out a photo is much easier with the new Straighten tool 🖳. Before beginning the exercise on page 47, you need to know a few things about the Straighten tool. To align an image horizontally, use the tool to draw a line in the image that should be horizontal. If there is no horizontal reference you can use a vertical reference; just hold down the Ctrl key and draw a line along something in the photo that should be vertical.

Figure 3.13
Is this photo crooked? With gas that cheap—who cares?

There are three options in the Tool Options bar that control what happens to the image after it is rotated: Grow Canvas to Fit, Crop to Remove Background, and Crop to Original Size. As you rotate any image, the dimensions of the photo increase or some pixels in the image must be cropped. **Figures 3.14–3.16** on this page and the next show the effects of these options.

Figure 3.14
The result of using the Grow Canvas to Fit Straighten tool option.

Figure 3.15
The result of using the Crop to Remove Background option.

Figure 3.16
The result of using the Crop to Original Size option.

Straightening a Crooked Photo

For our Straighten tool exercise I have a classic example of a crooked photo that needs to be straightened. The photo was taken from a car while waiting for a light to change.

1. Open the image **Crooked_photo.jpg** from the Peachpit Press Web site.

2. Select the Straighten tool (P) from the Toolbox. Change the option to Crop to Remove Background.

3. Hold down the Ctrl key, drag a line like the green line shown in **Figure 3.17**, and release. The Washington Monument (**Figure 3.18**, next page) appears straighter—or does it? In fact it is now leaning slightly to the right. Also notice the top of the obelisk is touching the top of the photo.

4. Undo the last action (Ctrl+Z) and apply the Straighten tool again by Ctrl-dragging a line as shown in **Figure 3.19**, next page. Your end point should be almost half the distance between the starting edge and the middle. This time it works and the cap of the monument isn't touching the sky (**Figure 3.20**, page 49).

So, what happened during the exercise and how did I pick the vertical line that I had you use? First of all, the Washington Monument isn't crooked but it was near the edge of the landscape in the photo. Barrel distortion produced by the wide-angle lens makes the obelisk appear to be bending in just like the buildings on the edge of the Chicago street scene in **Figure 3.21**, page 49. How did I pick the line to use? Experimentation. The Straighten tool works very fast, so it only took a few tries.

Drag the Straighten tool along this line.

Figure 3.17
Ctrl-drag the Straighten tool along the center vertical line.

Figure 3.18
Now the monument is tilting the other direction.

Figure 3.19
Ctrl-drag the Straighten tool along the center vertical line as directed.

Figure 3.20
Now the monument appears straight.

Buildings appear to lean in.

Figure 3.21
Barrel lens distortion makes the buildings on the edge of a photo appear to be bending inward.

Quick Fix: One-Stop Image Correction

The Editor contains two modes of operation—Standard Edit and Quick Fix.

Clicking the Quick Fix button in the Standard Edit mode switches over to the Quick Fix mode (**Figure 3.22**), taking over the entire screen (**Figure 3.23**). From here you can do just about everything related to image enhancement, including rotation, cropping, red-eye removal, and color and lighting adjustments. It even has Auto Smart Fix, which was introduced in Chapter 2. The Quick Fix mode takes sort of a Swiss Army knife approach to image correction and, like that famous knife, it has more features on it than you may ever use.

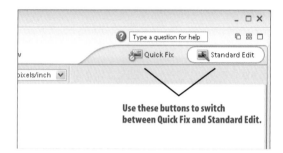

Figure 3.22

The Quick Fix and Standard Edit buttons are used to switch between editing modes.

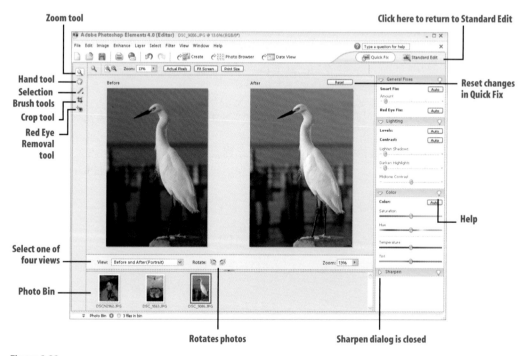

Figure 3.23

The Quick Fix dialog.

The Quick Fix Layout

Most of the tools shown in Figure 3.23 are self-explanatory but there are a few that should be noted.

- **View.** This feature allows you to select one of the four display views (**Figure 3.24**). The Before and After view is your best choice because you can see the changes being made. Make sure to use the orientation that matches your photo. If you choose otherwise, Elements makes the preview areas much smaller so they fit the chosen orientation, making them much harder to see.

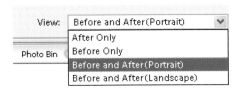

Figure 3.24
The View options for Quick Fix.

- **Photo Bin.** When more than one image is opened in Quick Fix the other pictures appear in the Photo Bin. Unlike the Photo Bin of the Standard Editor, you cannot minimize images in Quick Fix. See the sidebar "Taming the Wild Photo Bin" for information on how to use the Photo Bin in the Editor.

- **Reset.** The Reset button clears all of the changes made to the image you are working on. There are two ways to make changes: either click one of the Auto buttons or change one of the slider adjustments and click the Commit icon. If you just want to undo one of the adjustments made with a slider, click the Cancel icon (**Figure 3.25**) Please note that the Commit and Cancel icons do not appear until a change has been made to one of the sliders. The Reset button remains dim until either a slider adjustment is made and the Commit icon is clicked, or an Auto button is clicked.

TIP

Close the Photo Bin to have an even, large preview area.

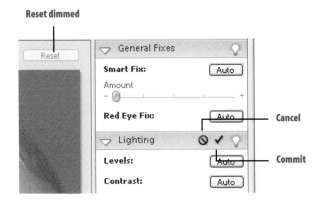

Reset dimmed

Figure 3.25
The Reset button and the Commit and Cancel icons.

Taming the Wild Photo Bin

Usually, most users' first encounter with the Photo Bin is by accident. Typically, when the cursor gets too close to the bottom of the Windows workspace, the Photo Bin suddenly pops open seemingly out of nowhere. The Photo Bin is a handy space that allows multiple images to be open without cluttering the Elements workspace. Here are some simple rules so you can understand how it works and how to use it:

- All open images that are minimized go to the Photo Bin.

- The Photo Bin can be minimized and opened from the Window menu (Window, Photo Bin). It can also be opened and closed by clicking on the icon in the lower-left corner of the Photo Bin (the icon is there even when it is closed).

- To prevent the Photo Bin from popping open every time your pointer gets in the lower part of your workspace, right-click on the Photo Bin and uncheck auto-hide.

Enhancing a Lifeless Photo

Many times I have taken a photo of something that really got my attention at the time I took the picture, but when I look at the image later, I am disappointed and question what ever prompted me to take the photo in the first place. Let's see how Elements can put some life back into a lifeless photo.

1. From the Peachpit Press Web site, download the image **Heron.jpg** and open it in Elements.

2. Click the Quick Fix button in the upper-right corner of the Editor.

3. Change the View to Before and After (Portrait), and then choose Fit On Screen (Ctrl+0).

4. Click at the point shown (**Figure 3.26**) in the Auto Fix section, and the image will immediately improve.

5. Click the Auto button in the Sharpen section, and the image is done.

If you click the Standard Edit button, you will return to the Standard Edit mode of the Editor. Notice that the adjustments applied in the Quick Fix mode now appear in the Undo History palette (**Figure 3.27**). The before and after appears in **Figure 3.28**.

TIP

While Auto Smart Fix is available from the Enhance menu in Editor, the advantage of applying it in Quick Fix mode is that the level of Smart Fix that is applied can be controlled if applied from the Quick Fix menu.

Click here to return to the Editor.

Click here to apply Smart Fix.

Click Auto to apply sharpening.

Figure 3.26
Using the Before and After (Portrait) view. Apply Smart Fix as shown.

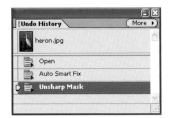

Figure 3.27
Undo History reflects all of the changes made in Quick Fix.

Figure 3.28
Quick Fix quickly brings life to an otherwise dull photo.

Shedding Light on Dark Photos

Quick Fix can be used to recover underexposed photographs, like the one shown in **Figure 3.29**. This type of problem is quite common. It is a bright sunny day which is producing a dark shadow on the model's face. As a result the outside area is properly exposed but the area under the hat is very dark. This exercise uses the photo **Man_with_hat.jpg** from the Peachpit Press Web site.

Figure 3.29
A hat on a sunny day hides the face in the shadows.

1. Open **Man_with_hat.jpg** in Elements, and open Quick Fix.

2. Move the Lighten Shadows slider to the position indicated in **Figure 3.30**. The man's face is now visible.

3. Return to Standard Edit by clicking the Standard Edit button. The shadow is gone but portions of his face are still dark (**Figure 3.31**). Select the Dodge tool and change the Tool Options setting as shown in **Figure 3.32** (page 56). Lightly apply the Dodge tool to lighten his face.

Figure 3.30
A heavy application of the Lighten Shadows command.

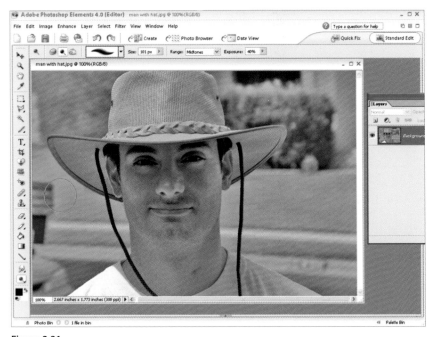

Figure 3.31
The face is lightened by Quick Fix but it still needs to have the darker portions of the face lightened.

Brush size   Range   Exposure

Dodge tool

Figure 3.32
The Dodge tool removes the last of the darkened areas.

Figure 3.33 shows the before and after of this photo.

Figure 3.33
Lighten Shadows has been applied in Quick Fix with great results.

Auto Contrast Vs. Auto Levels

These two automatic tools at times act in contradictory ways, so here is a brief explanation of how they work and differ to help you get the most out of using them. Auto Contrast redistributes the pixels between shadows and highlights, which improves the photo without affecting the colors. Auto Levels does the same thing, except it redistributes the pixels on each color channel individually, which usually produces a color shift—in most cases toward blue. So if you want to improve contrast without affecting the color, use Auto Contrast. Depending on the color composition of the image, Auto Levels can sometimes do a better job than Auto Contrast. The only way to know is to try it. If it doesn't work, click Undo.

The Auto Levels and Auto Contrast tools can be accessed in Quick Fix mode, and from the Enhance menu when in Standard Edit mode.

Getting the Red Out

Red eye is a problem that occurs often in flash photos—even though your camera may have a red eye reduction feature (see the sidebar "What Causes Red Eye?"). It is a problem that can make even a sweet young girl (**Figure 3.34**) look as if she is possessed.

Figure 3.34
A serious problem of red eye.

Fortunately, Adobe's newest incarnation of the Red Eye Removal tool in Elements makes the correction of red eye a very simple job, as you will discover in the next exercise. You will need to download the image **Red_eye.jpg** from the Peachpit Press Web page. The Red Eye Removal tool is available in both Quick Fix and Standard Edit mode.

1. From the Standard Edit mode, open the photograph **Red_eye.jpg**.

2. Select the Red Eye Removal tool (Y) in the Toolbox (**Figure 3.35**, next page).

3. With the Options bar set to the default values (both are 50 percent), click on the red part of one eye. After a moment the red will be replaced with a much darker color. Repeat with the other eye. The red eye is gone (**Figure 3.36**, next page).

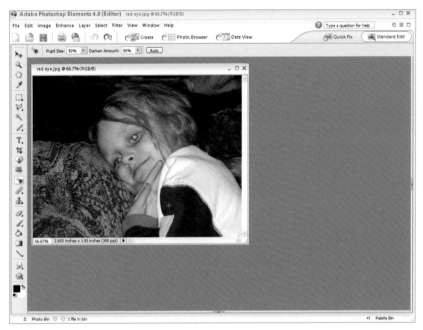

Figure 3.35
The Auto Red Eye Removal tool.

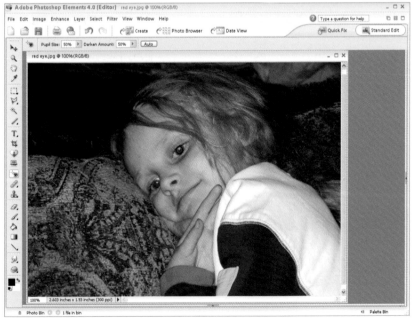

Figure 3.36
Red eye removed in two strokes.

What Causes Red Eye?

Red Eye occurs when taking photos of people or animals using flash lighting. It never happens with natural lighting (from the sun). Factors that produce red eye in your final picture are when the angle between flash and camera lens is too narrow or the ambient lighting is too dim (or your subject has had a few drinks). This explains why photos of a bunch of men on a hunting trip, as they are sitting around a campfire, can produce examples of red eye that look like a scene from a sci-fi movie. The reason for increased incidence of red eye when the subject is in the dark is that the subject's pupil has dilated to adjust to the darker environment. So when you take a flash photo, the light from the flash reflects off of the retina in the back of the eye. The light is reflected and is picked up by the camera. What you are actually seeing is the reflection of blood in the eye.

Sharpening—The Last Step

After you are happy with the color and other adjustments that you made to the photo, you should sharpen it. Here are a few things to know about sharpening photos:

- If the photo is out of focus, after you apply sharpening it will still be out of focus.

- Photoshop Elements (and Photoshop) offers several different types of sharpening. Make it a habit to use the Unsharp Mask (see the sidebar, "Unsharp Mask: Great Tool with a Weird Name"). The Auto setting for sharpening in Auto Fix uses the Unsharp Mask.

- Apply sharpening last, after you have performed other adjustments to your photos.

- If you are going to change the size of the image, don't apply sharpening until you have the image at its final size.

How Sharp Is Sharp Enough?

How much sharpening should you apply? It depends on what you are sharpening. If you are sharpening a portrait of a middle-aged person, sharpening will bring out all the details (wrinkles) in his or her face, so you wouldn't necessarily want too much, if any, sharpening. If you are applying sharpening to man-made objects, such as buildings or cars, you can get away with almost any amount. You know you have applied too much sharpening when lighter parts of the image begin to lose their details and become solid white. This phenomenon is called a blowout and should be avoided.

Unsharp Mask: Great Tool with a Weird Name

The term Unsharp Mask is actually the name for the original process, which dates back almost one hundred years. There are two Unsharp Mask filters in Elements. In the Quick Fix mode, it is a single slider with an Auto button. In Standard Edit mode, it is in the Filter menu under Sharpen. You will discover Unsharp Mask at the bottom of the drop-down list of all the other Sharpen filters. The three dots (ellipsis) that follow the name indicate that a dialog is associated with the filter. (Of the Sharpen filters, only the Unsharp Mask filter has a dialog.)

When the Unsharp Mask dialog appears, you'll see three adjustment sliders: Amount, Radius, and Threshold. Three controls that interact with each other can seem complicated, so for most sharpening, I recommend that you keep the Threshold at 0, the Radius at a value of 1, and begin with the Amount slider at 100 percent and move it until the image looks right. If you are working on really large images (made by a 4+ megapixel camera), you may consider increasing the radius to a value of 2.

The Best Zoom for Previewing Effects

When you are viewing the photo on your computer screen at anything other than 100 percent, the image that you see is not an accurate representation of the actual photo. Without getting too technical, at all zoom settings other than 100 percent (called Actual Pixels, in Elements), the computer is not showing you the actual pixels in the image. To create the requested viewing zoom level, the computer is making an approximation of the pixels.

Although viewing at this zoom level might not fit on your screen, always change the viewing to the Actual Pixels when evaluating critical changes. You can select Actual Pixels in the Options bar after the Zoom tool has been selected, or you can use the keyboard shortcut Alt+Ctrl+0.

Another potential problem occurs when sharpening a scanned photograph, negative, or slide: sharpening emphasizes all the dust, hair, and other debris on the photo or scanner glass. **Figure 3.37** shows part of a photograph scanned using a flatbed scanner. If you look close you can see the debris that was embedded in the print.

This debris is especially noticeable if a photo has many dark areas, such as a dark suit or dress worn by someone in the photo. Applying too much sharpening to Figure 3.37 produces a snowstorm of junk (**Figure 3.38**). (To demonstrate a point and create the image shown in Figure 3.38, I applied the Unsharp Mask at an insane setting—Radius of 6 at 200%.)

Sometimes even a moderate amount of sharpening can light up all the debris that you should have cleaned off the photograph or scanner before scanning.

NOTE

Problems caused by over sharpening are more apparent in black-and-white (grayscale) photographs than those in color.

Figure 3.37
Scanned photo has a lot of debris on it.

Figure 3.38
Over sharpening can make all of the junk on a photo stand out.

Now that you know how to do the quick and slick photo fixups, the next chapter deals with the all-important topic of color and how to remove unwanted color casts, plus a lot of other color issues.

Color Challenges and Solutions

In the previous chapters we learned how to solve some of the more common problems faced with digital photography. In this chapter, you will discover basic techniques used to correct, enhance, and even change colors in your photos. The chapter is divided into three major sections: Automatic color correction, manual color correction, and the fun part—color manipulation. We will start with the automatic tools.

Calibrating Your Monitor

Before we can begin working seriously with color, you may want to ensure the colors in your monitor are calibrated. Without calibrating the colors in your monitor, you may waste a lot of time fine-tuning colors in your image only to see a completely different set of colors displayed when the image appears on another monitor or is printed. Color mis-match problems are especially acute when using older CRT monitors because the color phosphors inside a CRT change with age.

There are two ways to calibrate your monitor: You can use a software-only approach, or you can use an external calibration device in combination with your monitor. See the sidebar, "Monitor Calibration Solutions."

Why Calibrate?

Monitor color calibration is not just for professionals. If you take the 5-10 minutes required to run the calibration software provided by Adobe, you will stand a better chance of receiving color prints that look closer to what you see on the screen than if you didn't calibrate. Calibrating your monitor will not rejuvenate an aging monitor or restore the colors in a monitor in which one of the color guns isn't working properly. The difference when you are finished calibrating may be great or barely noticeable (which means your monitor was spot on when you began). What is important is that you have a known starting point for the colors with which you are working.

There is a wizard-style calibration routine available to calibrate the colors in your CRT monitor called Adobe Gamma (Adobe does not recommend using Adobe Gamma on LCD-flat panel-monitors). It was installed in your system at the time you installed Elements. If you had an older version of Adobe Gamma already installed, it was replaced with the new version when you installed Elements.

Defining Accurate Color Using Adobe Gamma

While Adobe Gamma is a wizard-style application, I have included some basic information about starting and using it. Here is how to calibrate your monitor:

1. Go to Start, Control Panel. When the window opens, switch the Control Panel view to Classic view, and choose Adobe Gamma (**Figure 4.1**). This launches the Adobe Gamma window (**Figure 4.2**). Choose Step By Step (Wizard) and click Next.

2. In the Description text box, the name that appears should be the name of the color profile installed for your monitor. You can also type in your own name for the profile (I recommend a name such as the brand of monitor you are using and the date).

Change View here.

Double-click here.

Figure 4.1
Select Classic View of Control Panel to access Adobe Gamma

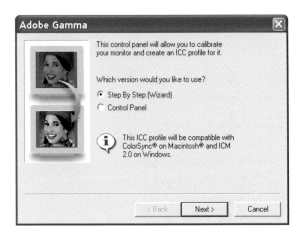

Figure 4.2
Use the Step By Step (Wizard) for calibrating your CRT monitor.

3. The next screen is for setting up contrast and adjusting brightness (**Figure 4.3**). Just make sure your brightness is set to maximum. When you have made the adjustments, click Next.

4. Selecting phosphors comes next (**Figure 4.4**). You can choose from a long list of monitors with strange-sounding names, but unless you can actually find your specific monitor profile, go with Trinitron for a CRT monitor and click Next.

Figure 4.3
Adjust Contrast and Brightness.

Figure 4.4
Pick a phosphor setting for your CRT monitor.

5. The Gamma setting has two options (**Figure 4.5**). You can make the adjustment using a single gray screen, or you can adjust each color channel individually. My recommendation is to use the single gray color swatch if your monitor is relatively new, and the individual channels if your CRT is over two years old. That's because the color balance between individual color channels in an older CRT monitor are more likely to change. To adjust the Gamma, you need to squint your eyes (no kidding) and adjust the sliders until the colors (or the background and foreground of the gray color swatch) appear to blend. They won't be exactly the same but get them as close as possible. Don't change the Windows Default setting. Click Next.

6. One of the last screens (**Figure 4.6**, next page) lets you pick the Hardware White Point, which means you are determining if you want areas of pure white to have a cooler (slightly bluish), neutral, or warmer (slightly redder) appearance. You can even click the Measure button, which will open another screen with instructions on how select the white point. I recommend taking the default (which is the neutral setting) and moving to the next screen (not shown), which just confirms that you want to use the white point you selected in the previous screen.

7. From this screen, you can see the change produced by the profile you just created by clicking the Before and After button (**Figure 4.7**, next page). As you click between them, the effect of the original or the profile you just created controls the screen appearance. If you want to change some of the choices you made, use the Back button and make the changes. If you are satisfied with the new profile, click Next, and you will be asked to name the new color profile before saving it.

That's it! You are all calibrated. It took less than five minutes and it was free.

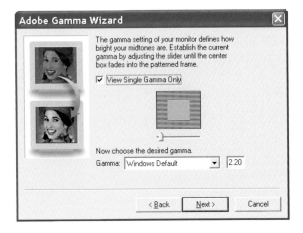

Figure 4.5
The Gamma setting is used to balance the colors to produce accurate, neutral colors, which is important.

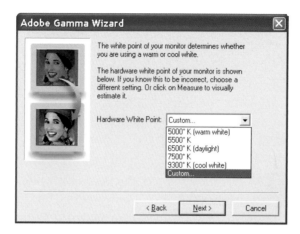

Figure 4.6
Selecting the white point controls the overall cooler or warmer appearance of images on your screen.

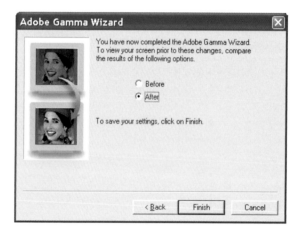

Figure 4.7
From this screen you can compare the appearance of the original and the calibrated color profile.

Tackling Color Casts with Automatic Features

One of the more difficult and common color challenges is correcting a color cast in a photo. A color cast is a shift of the overall color in an image toward cooler or warmer colors. If you are outside on a bright sunny summer day, everything you see has a bluish tint to it. It's true, but you don't notice it because your brain filters it out and the colors seem normal. Your camera isn't as smart as your built-in optical system, so the camera captures all the colors present, including those that you don't want. See the sidebar, "Accurate vs. Desired Colors."

Correcting Color in Photos with People

One of the best automatic tools for correcting colors in a photo that contains people is a new addition to Photoshop Elements—Adjust Color for Skin Tone. It makes the skin color of people in a photo look better and it corrects all of the other colors at the same time. If you want to try it out, download the image **Young_woman.jpg** from the Peachpit Press Web site.

1. Open **Young_woman.jpg** (**Figure 4.8**).

Figure 4.8
The original photo has a blue color cast.

2. Choose Enhance, Adjust Color, Adjust Color for Skin Tone, which opens a dialog (**Figure 4.9**, next page).

3. Place the cursor over the photo and it becomes an eyedropper. Click on the woman's skin and immediately the photo loses its blue color cast (**Figure 4.10**, next page). Click OK and you are finished.

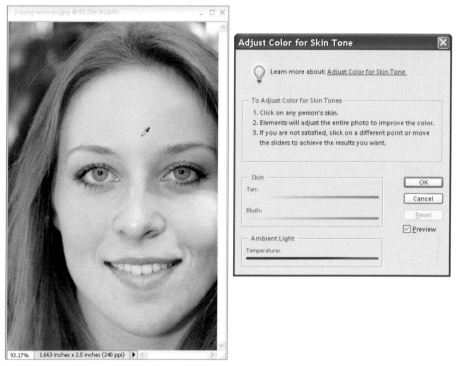

Figure 4.9
The Adjust Color for Skin Tone dialog.

The change in the color is subtle, which is what it should be. Many photos that have strong color casts need just a little adjustment to correct them. There are other fun things you can do with the Adjust Color for Skin Tone feature, which are covered later in this chapter.

Here are some tips about using Adjust Color for Skin Tone:

- Experiment using different areas of skin as a sample point and see which produces the desired effect. Avoid exceptionally bright or dark areas of skin.

- Often the colors in the preview will appear to be warm (reddish-orange). When this happens, try moving the Ambient Light slider at the bottom of the dialog to the left. Move it just a small amount.

- If you are working on an exceptionally large image—that is, a photo from a camera using a 5 megapixel sensor or larger—give the preview a few seconds to refresh the preview before moving the slider again.

- You will notice the Tan and Blush sliders have very little effect on the photo. They are designed to produce very subtle changes and should only be used to fine-tune.

Figure 4.10
In a single step the color cast is corrected.

Auto Color Correction

Found in the Enhance menu, the Auto Color Correction tool is described in the Photoshop Elements User Guide as a command that "Adjusts the contrast and color by identifying shadows, midtones, and highlights in the image, rather than in individual color channels. It neutralizes the midtones and clips the white and black pixels using a default set of values." While the Auto Color Correction command improves with each release of Photoshop Elements, in many cases it will introduce a slight color cast when applied, or it may throw the colors off completely, and other times it will work as designed. To demonstrate, you can download the file **Sunflowers.jpg** from the Peachpit Press Web site.

1. Open **Sunflowers.jpg** (**Figure 4.11**, next page).

2. Choose Enhance, Adjust Color, Auto Color Correction (Shift+Ctrl+B) (**Figure 4.12**, next page).

   The result is an unwanted magenta color shift, as shown in **Figure 4.13**.

3. Close the file. Don't save changes but remember where the file is located because we will be using it later.

Figure 4.11
This field of sunflowers has several color problems.

Figure 4.12
Selecting the Auto Color Correction tool.

Figure 4.13
The Auto Color Correction tool makes the colors worse.

How do you know when to use the Auto Color Correction? My advice is to try it (its operation is almost instantaneous) and it if doesn't work, Undo the command (Ctrl+Z) and move on to a different color adjustment tool.

Additional Color Fixer-Upper Tools

Now that you have seen the purely automatic tools, let's look at some other tools for correcting or enhancing color when the automatic tools don't work. The first one we will look at is Remove Color Cast.

Removing Shadows and Color Casts

To do this exercise, download the file **Oriental_garden.jpg** from the Peachpit Press Web site.

1. Open the file **Oriental_garden.jpg** (**Figure 4.14**). Before adjusting the color, we should first correct the tonal deficiencies of the photo (there are soft shadows under the stone pagoda). Choose Enhance, Adjust Lighting, Shadows/Highlights (**Figure 4.15**). The Shadows/Highlights dialog opens.

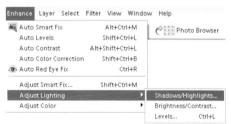

Figure 4.14
This photo taken on an overcast day has a blue color cast.

Figure 4.15
The first step is to apply Shadows/Highlights.

2. Accept the default settings (**Figure 4.16**) and click OK. The shadows are diminished (**Figure 4.17**) and now the photo is ready for color adjustment.

3. Choose Enhance, Adjust Color, Remove Color Cast (**Figure 4.18**).

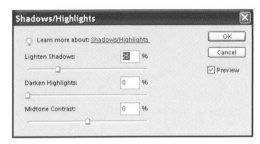

Figure 4.16
The default setting of Shadows/Highlights works in most cases.

Figure 4.17
Once the shadow areas have been softened the color cast is more apparent.

4. When the dialog opens, place the cursor (which becomes an eyedropper) over one of the points indicated in **Figure 4.19**. I chose these points because they are areas that are closest to neutral gray in the photo. Each time you click on any part of the pagoda the color balance of the entire image shifts. When you have it the way you like it (**Figure 4.20**), click OK and you're finished—or are you?

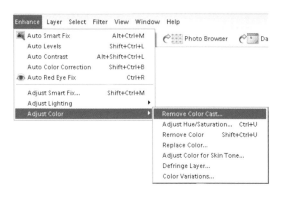

Figure 4.18
Good subject, diffused lighting (no harsh shadows), but the overcast skies make the color in the image appear flat.

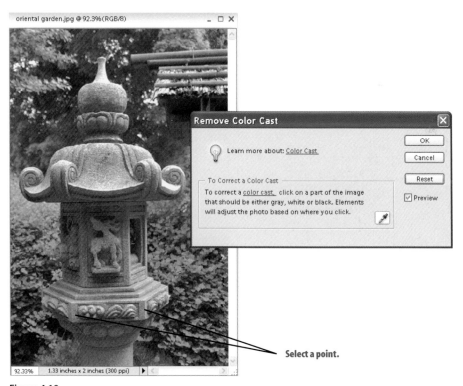

Select a point.

Figure 4.19
Click on the neutral gray areas as samples for Remove Color Cast.

Figure 4.20
The color cast is gone but the colors look a little dull.

How to Use the Remove Color Cast Command

Remove Color Cast works on a simple principle. You look at the photo and determine what color should be neutral (white, black, or gray). When you click the eyedropper cursor of the Remove Color Cast tool on a spot of color that you think is neutral, Elements calculates the color cast by reading the color that you selected as neutral, and generates what it thinks is the color adjustment correction necessary to remove the color cast. That's if you pick the right color.

Here are some areas to avoid when selecting samples. Don't include dark shadows and bright spots of white (blowouts). Typically you don't want to select any part of an image's border, but if you have a photograph that has changed colors with age, sampling its originally white border works great. If the first point you sample doesn't work, click the Reset button in the dialog and try another. Be aware that there are some images that have no usable neutral colors and in such cases this tool won't work. When that happens, don't waste a lot of time trying to make it work, move on to another method.

Using Hue/Saturation

Look at the color-adjusted photo (Figure 4.20). The blue cast caused by the overcast sky is gone but all of the background greenery appears flat. Here is a quick remedy:

1. Open the Hue/Saturation dialog by using the command Ctrl+U.

2. Select Greens in the Edit section (**Figure 4.21**). Place the cursor (which again becomes an eyedropper) over the green leaves behind the pagoda in the photo and click on a leaf. Notice what changes in the dialog—the Edit setting is changed to Yellows 2 after the color is sampled. Also note that the selected color range now appears on the bottom sliders (**Figure 4.22**). We will learn more about this when we fix the sunflower photo.

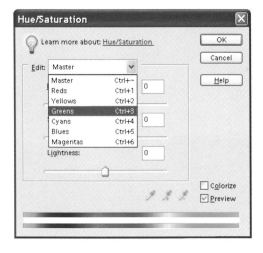

Figure 4.21
The Greens Edit selection in the Hue/Saturation dialog.

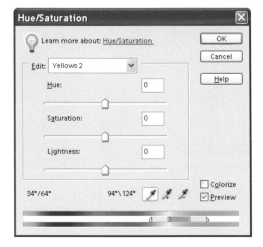

Figure 4.22
Sampling the greenery in the photo makes the range of selected color appear on the bottom of the dialog.

3. To verify that the selected colors are those that we want to change, drag the Saturation slider all the way to the left. All of the greenery becomes grayscale (**Figure 4.23**). Now move the slider back to the right until it is about +40 and click OK. The greens look more vivid (**Figure 4.24**).

Figure 4.23
Slide the Saturation slider to the left to see what colors are selected.

Figure 4.24
The greens appear much more vivid.

Using the Sponge Tool

The bamboo structure in the background really looks colorless, here is a quick trick to add color to it:

1. Select the Sponge tool.

2. Change the Tool Options settings to Mode: Saturate, Flow: 75% and paint the bamboo structure in the background. **Figure 4.25** shows the before and after image.

Figure 4.25
Apply the Sponge tool to the building to bring out some additional colors.

Correcting the Sunny Day Blues

Another great tool used for color correction in Elements is the Color Variations tool. The following exercise teaches you how to use the Color Variations tool to correct a bluish color cast using the photo **Blue_cast_church.jpg** from the Peachpit Press Web site. A bright blue sky and a bright white siding often produce a blue cast like the one in the photo.

1. Open the image **Blue_cast_church.jpg**. This photo (**Figure 4.26**, next page) was taken on a bright sunny afternoon with a cloudless sky. The reflection of the blue sky produces a bluish cast on the entire image.

2. Choose Enhance, Adjust Color, Color Variations to open the Color Variations dialog (**Figure 4.27**, next page).

3. Click the Increase Red preview thumbnail, click the Lighten thumbnail, and then click OK. The blue color cast is removed although the white church still isn't the bright white that I took when I shot the photo (**Figure 4.28**, next page).

Figure 4.26
Photographing a white building on a sunny day produces unwanted color casts.

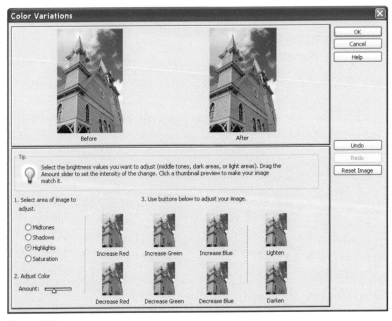

Figure 4.27
The Color Variations dialog.

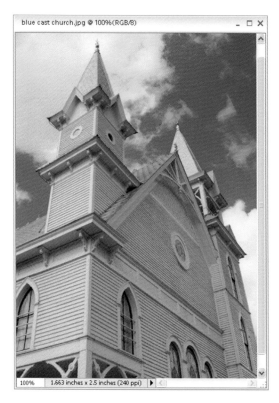

blue cast church.jpg @ 100%(RGB/8)

100%   1.663 inches x 2.5 inches (240 ppi)

Figure 4.28
After applying Color Variations, the blue cast is gone but some colors still are not correct.

Understanding How Colors Work

So, why didn't we use Auto Color Correction as we did earlier in the chapter? Because if you use it or Remove Color Cast with the photo used in the previous exercise, there will be little to no change (try it). Unlike the other color correction tools, Color Variations

Colors and Their Opposites

You may know that digital color images are composed of three primary colors, Red, Green and Blue (RGB), which appear at the bottom of the Color Variations dialog (Figure 4.27). What you may not know is that each primary color has an opposite color (called a secondary color): They are, respectively, Cyan, Magenta, and Yellow (CMY). The secondary colors are listed in the Color Variations dialog as Decrease Red (cyan), Decrease Green (magenta), and Decrease Blue (yellow) at the bottom of the Color Variations. The relationship between colors is as follows:

- Increase Red to decrease Cyan, decrease Red to increase Cyan

- Increase Green to decrease Magenta, decrease Green to increase Magenta

- Increase Blue to decrease Yellow, decrease Blue to increase Yellow

is not an automatic tool and it requires that you make decisions about which color to change. To do that successfully means you need to understand a little about how colors act and react with one another (see the sidebar, "Colors and Their Opposites" to learn more).

The color cast in the photo (Figure 4.26) appears as a faded blue, indicating it most likely is a cyan color cast, and not blue. This is why we added Red to the photo in the previous exercise, to reduce the cyan in the photo. The main problem with Color Variations is the small size of the preview thumbnails and the inability to zoom in on the Before and After previews.

Correcting Color Balance in a Raw Image

To be fair, the photo of the church was taken as a Raw file and to provide the image that you worked on in the last exercise, I opened the image but didn't apply any color correction. Raw file format is covered in the appendix of this book, but for now here is how to correct the colors in a Raw image. Due to the size of the Raw image (>6 MB) a sample file is not available for download.

1. Open a Raw file. This launches the Camera Raw plug-in dialog (**Figure 4.29**).

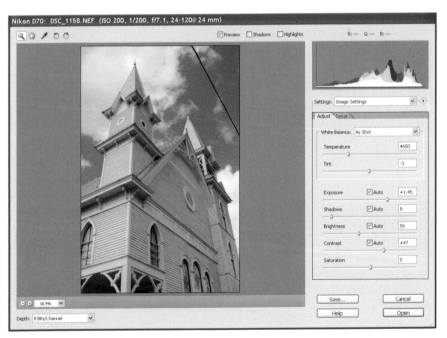

Figure 4.29
The Camera Raw plug-in dialog.

2. Select the White Balance eyedropper tool and click on a part of the image that is supposed to be white (**Figure 4.30**). Do not click on a reflection. You might think that the clouds would be a good choice but they are highly reflective so instead click on the part of the church that is white.

This action automatically corrects the white balance of the photo and removes any unwanted color cast. (In case you were wondering about the black line... it is a power line that I removed from the file used in the previous example.)

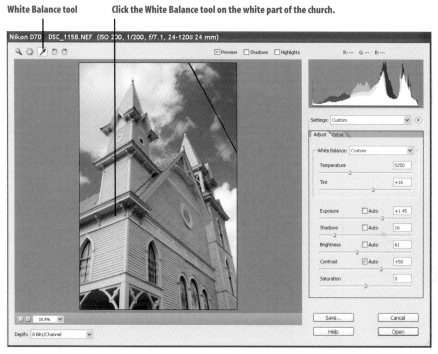

Figure 4.30
Using auto White Balance corrects all of the colors in the Camera Raw plug-in dialog.

Other Causes of Color Casts

If you notice that the images you bring in from your digital camera have a consistent reddish or greenish cast, then the color space information provided by your camera may be causing the problem. See the sidebar "What Is EXIF Camera Data?" for more information. To see if this is the cause of your color casts, change the camera data EXIF settings in Preferences. Here is how it's done:

1. Choose Edit, Preferences, Saving Files (**Figure 4.31**).

2. Check Ignore Camera Data (EXIF) profiles and click OK.

By having Elements ignore the EXIF data settings your image isn't altered in any way. It is just telling Elements to either use the EXIF color information or not in calculating the way Elements displays the image. It does not affect any of the EXIF data (type of camera, date photo was taken, camera settings).

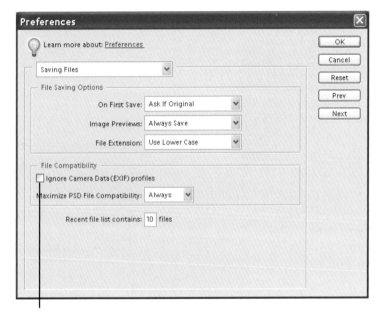

Click here.

Figure 4.31
Ignoring Camera Data (EXIF) helps prevent color mismatch problems.

What Is EXIF Camera Data?

Besides the photo, nearly all cameras store additional information such as the date and time the image was taken, aperture, shutter speed, ISO, and most other camera settings. This data, also known as "metadata," is stored in a special file called the EXIF (Exchangeable Image File) header. EXIF data are very useful because you do not need to worry about remembering the settings you used when taking the image. Later you can analyze on your computer which camera settings created the best results, so you can learn from your experience. If you're not familiar with the term colorspace, it is a complicated mathematical model used to define how colors appear. The EXIF standard only allows two values for the EXIF colorspace: sRGB or NONE. The sRGB colorspace of some camera manufacturers is different from the sRGB in Elements. When this happens it causes colors to display inaccurately, often appearing as a red or greenish color cast. To prevent this, you must set Elements to ignore the EXIF color information.

Checklist for Fixing Color Casts

When trying to correct an unwanted color cast, here is a recommended order of things to try:

1. **Adjust Color for Skin Tone**. Use if people are in the photo. In many cases this solves the problem.

2. **Auto Contrast**. Apply the Auto Contrast first. Sometimes (not often) this corrects the problem.

3. **Auto Color Correction**. This works most often when there are large amounts of white in the image. If it doesn't work, Undo (Ctrl+Z) it, and go to the next step.

4. **Remove Color Cast**. If Auto Color Correction didn't work, there is a good chance Remove Color Cast won't work either, but you should give it a try if the photo has small areas of white in it.

5. **Color Variations**. This is the tool of last resort. Experiment with it, trying different combinations of colors, and adding changes to Highlights and Shadows on the left side of the dialog.

Adding a Color Cast for Effect

Sometimes you will want to add an overlay color (color cast) to produce an effect. For example, you can add a color tint to make a photo look old or rustic. To do this exercise, you will need to download the file **Old_lantern.jpg** from the Peachpit Web site. Adding a color cast is done using the Colorize option of the Hue/Saturation command. Here is how to do it:

1. Open the file **Old_lantern.jpg** (**Figure 4.32**, next page).

2. Open the Hue/Saturation dialog by using command Ctrl+U.

Accurate Colors Vs. Desired Colors

When correcting or enhancing colors in a photo, there are two general schools of thought: The first is, make the colors accurate so the colors in the photo appear exactly as they appeared when you shot the photo. The other approach is to enhance or correct the colors in the photo so they appear as you imagine they should appear. Photojournalists are strong advocates of accurate color. They eschew any attempts to alter the reality expressed by the photo. Nearly everyone else just wants their photos to look good when they show them to others, and so any color changes that make the photo look better are acceptable. So if you're not a photojournalist, have fun enhancing, changing, and replacing colors in your photos, and don't let anyone make you feel guilty about doing it—even a photojournalist.

3. Click the Colorize check box. Moving the Hue slider controls what color the overall image will have, while the Saturation slider determines how much or how little of the color tint will be applied. For this exercise, choose a Hue setting of 50 and a Saturation setting of 25 (**Figure 4.33**). In most cases you will not change the Lightness setting. Click OK to apply the change (**Figure 4.34**).

4. As a finishing touch, give the photo an antique appearance by choosing Filter, Artistic, Poster Edges and apply the setting as shown in **Figure 4.35**.

Figure 4.32
A color photo of an old lantern.

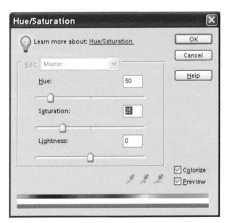

Figure 4.33
Use these settings in the Hue/Saturation dialog.

Figure 4.34
Using Colorize makes the photo appear to be an antique.

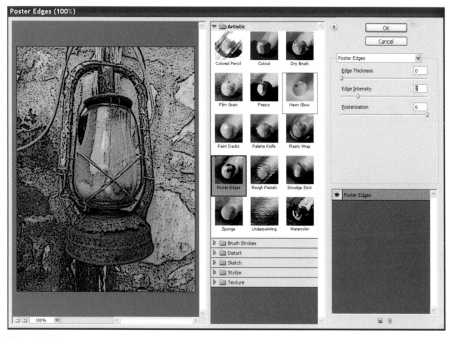

Figure 4.35
The Poster Edges filter gives it a final touch.

More Uses for Adjust Color For Skin Tone

I mentioned earlier in the chapter that the Adjust Color For Skin Tone tool wasn't limited to just working with skin. It is a great way to warm up an image with colors that are cool. To do this exercise you will need to download the image **Wood_lion.jpg** from the Peachpit Press Web site.

1. Open the image **Wood_lion.jpg** (**Figure 4.36**).

2. Choose Enhance, Adjust Color, Adjust Color for Skin Tone, which opens a dialog.

3. Click anywhere on the paws. The image will appear in a warmer tone, as shown in **Figure 4.37**. You can try different areas to see what other changes might be made. Note that you need to click the Reset button before selecting a different sample.

4. Use the sliders to change the amount and color of warmth being added to the image as shown in **Figure 4.38**.

Figure 4.36
This wooden lion has a great smile but cool colors.

Figure 4.37
Using the Adjust Color for Skin Tone tool creates a warmer image.

Figure 4.38
The effect of Adjust Color for Skin Tone
can be made warmer or cooler.

You can use this tool to correct the color in other images without people in them. To do this exercise you will need to download **Blue_cast_flower.jpg** from the Peachpit Press Web site. This photo was taken on a very bright sunny day in Texas. Because the flower is very small (several could fit on the head of a U.S. dime), I shot it in macro mode using an early model digital camera that had a tendency to go very blue on bright daylight shots.

1. Open the image **Blue_cast_flower.jpg** (**Figure 4.39**, next page).

2. Apply Auto Contrast (Enhance, Auto Contrast). This really brightens up the image (**Figure 4.40**, next page).

3. Open the Adjust Color for Skin Tone and click on the flower as shown in **Figure 4.41** (page 91). If the colors are too warm, you can move the Ambient Temperature slider to the left to make them cooler.

Figure 4.39
A macro photo of a small flower has color problems.

Figure 4.40
Applying Auto Contrast brightens up the image.

Figure 4.41
The effect of Adjust Color for Skin Tone brings the colors to life.

Replacing Colors

Photoshop Elements has a tool called Replace Color that can be really handy for times when you want to change a limited range of colors. The next exercise uses the file **Margarita_man.jpg**, which can be downloaded from the Peachpit Press Web site. There are many problems with this image. First there is a slight blue color cast. The bigger problems are **a)** he is holding a salted margarita glass that is the wrong color (ha! Real men don't drink strawberry margaritas), and **b)** the stem and base of the glass are a strange blue color.

Here is how to replace the colors in the photo:

1. Open the file **Margarita_man.jpg** (**Figure 4.42**).

2. Choose Enhance, Adjust Color, Adjust Color for Skin Tone, which opens a dialog. Click on the man's face to remove the blue color cast (**Figure 4.43**).

3. Next we need to make the margarita green but we don't want the cherry to become green as well. To isolate the color in the margarita, create an elliptical selection like the one shown in **Figure 4.44** (see Chapter 6 for more on selections).

Figure 4.42
This figure has a blue color cast, but what's worse is that the margarita is red.

Figure 4.43
Using the Adjust Color for Skin Tone tool to remove the blue color cast.

Selection

Figure 4.44
Create a selection around the red area.

4. Choose Enhance, Adjust Color, Replace Color, and the Replace Color dialog appears on the workspace. Change the Fuzziness setting to 60 (**Figure 4.45**).

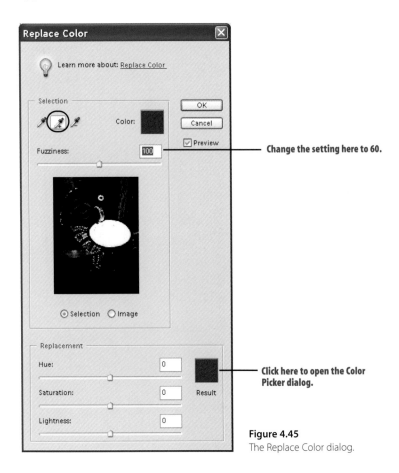

Change the setting here to 60.

Click here to open the Color Picker dialog.

Figure 4.45
The Replace Color dialog.

5. As you can see in the preview box, most of the red is already selected. To include the ripples, select the eyedropper with the plus sign beside it. Each time you click on an area, it gets included in the colors to be replaced. See the sidebar "Learning More About Using Color Replacement" for more information.

6. Once all of the red in the glass is selected, click on the Result color swatch. This opens the Color Picker dialog (**Figure 4.46**).

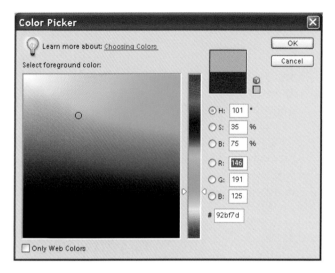

Figure 4.46
Pick out a margarita green to replace the red.

Figure 4.47
The replacement color looks better but there is more work to do.

7. Pick a color of green that you think appropriate for the margarita. Click OK and the drink is now the correct color. (**Figure 4.47**).

8. Deselect the image (Ctrl+D) and make a new rough selection around the stem and base of the glass as shown in **Figure 4.48**. Repeat the process in step 3 to isolate the colors in the base and stem. Rather than change the color, though, reduce the Saturation. Use the settings shown in **Figure 4.49**. The resulting image is shown in **Figure 4.50**.

I added some finishing touches in **Figure 4.51**. I used Replace Color to remove the black rim around the edge and replaced it with white. I then made a selection (explained in Chapter 6) around all of the margarita man and put him against a black background.

Figure 4.48
Create a rough selection around the base and stem of the glass.

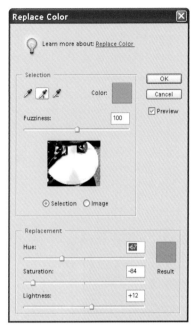

Figure 4.49
Use these settings to make the glass stem and base look more like glass.

Figure 4.50
One color cast removed and two colors replaced in a few simple operations.

Learning More About Using Color Replacement

There are two keys to using Color Replacement: selecting the existing color and creating the replacement color.

After selecting the initial color with the eyedropper cursor, there are several ways to increase the range of colors selected. Moving the Fuzziness slider to the right increases the range of colors to be replaced, while moving it to the left limits the range of colors selected for replacement. The small preview box indicates the areas of the photo that are selected. Areas that are white are selected, while the darker areas are not. The problem with increasing the range of selected colors using the Fuzziness slider is a tendency to include colors you don't want. The best way to increase the range of colors to be replaced is to hold down the Shift key while clicking on additional shades of the color you want to include for replacement. Conversely, holding down the Ctrl key while clicking on a color will remove the color from ones already selected.

Sometimes the colors selected aren't the ones you want included (for example, if the colors are selected because they are close in color to the desired colors). The easiest way to deal with this is by creating a rough selection with the Polygon Lasso tool in the Tools palette that excludes nearby areas of similar color.

There are two ways to define the replacement color. You can move the Hue, Saturation, and Lightness sliders until you get the combination you like. This technique will not work on white, black, or gray (they are all neutral colors). To select a specific color, click on the Result color swatch in the lower-right corner of the dialog, and the Color Picker dialog will open. From here you can find any color under the sun.

26.27%   6.4 inches x 8.533 inches (300 ppi)

Figure 4.51
Replacing the background makes the subject really stand out.

Putting It All Together

Remember that field of sunflowers that couldn't be fixed with Auto Color Correction back at the beginning of the chapter? Here is a way to really fix up the photo using several of the tools we learned in this chapter.

1. Open **Sunflowers.jpg**. Look at the photo (**Figure 4.52**). What's wrong with it? Look at the sky. We need to correct the color of blue in the sky.

2. Open the Hue/Saturation dialog by using the Ctrl+U command. Change the Edit setting to Blue and click in the upper-left corner of the sky. Change the settings to match those shown in **Figure 4.53**. Click OK. The clouds have reappeared and the blue looks more like a real sky blue (**Figure 4.54**).

3. In the Layers palette, add a new layer to the background by clicking the New Layer icon (**Figure 4.55**).

Figure 4.52
This is the field of sunflowers that Auto Color Correction couldn't correct.

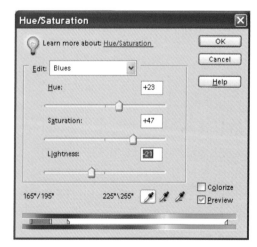

Figure 4.53
Use these settings to make the colors in the sky more realistic.

Figure 4.54
Selective color adjustment using Hue/Saturation makes the photo look better.

New Layer icon

Figure 4.55
Add a new layer over the background.

4. Change to the Default colors by pressing D. Select the Gradient tool and change the Tool Options setting of the Foreground to Transparent and the other settings as shown in **Figure 4.56**.

Figure 4.56
Use these Tool Options settings with the Gradient tool.

5. With the top layer selected, use the Gradient tool to drag a line straight down the middle of the photo. The result will look like **Figure 4.57**.

6. Change the Blending mode of the top layer to Soft Light (**Figure 4.58**).

7. Select the Background and use Hue/Saturation to add a little pop to the sunflowers (**Figure 4.59**). Flatten the image (Layer, Flatten Image) and increase Saturation (+15) using Hue/Saturation before applying Sharpening.

Figure 4.57
The Gradient layer makes the image darker.

Figure 4.58
Changing the Blending mode to Soft Light.

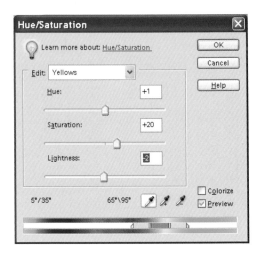

Figure 4.59
Select the yellow of the sunflowers.

The finished image shown in **Figure 4.60** (with corrected color) looks a lot more appealing than the original shot.

Figure 4.60
A photo that Kansas can be proud of.

There is so much more that you can do with color that it could fill an entire book. While this topic will appear in other sections of the book, for now you have learned enough to be creative with color in your photos and be able to solve a majority of your color-related problems. Now that you know how to fix all of these photos, in the next chapter you will discover how to organize them.

5 Organizing and Managing Your Pictures

One of the advantages of a digital camera is the freedom to take as many photos as you like without the additional costs of film and developing. This advantage can also turn into a nightmare unless you have a way to organize and manage your photos. With so many places for the photos to hide—external hard drives, Zip drives, CD-ROMs—it's a wonder that we can ever find the photo we are looking for. In this chapter, you will discover how to use the Organizer in Elements to organize your photos, and more importantly, how to locate a specific photo when you need it.

Basics of Image Organization

In Chapter 2 you learned that Photoshop Elements consists of an Organizer and an Editor. The Organizer does a lot of other things besides organizing your collection of photos but in this chapter we will be looking just at the tools used for bringing some order to your photo collection. Before we begin exploring the Organizer, we must first consider some ideas about general file organization of images.

Use Folders to Categorize Photos

Regardless of the tools that you choose to organize your photos, I strongly recommend that you keep photos categorized in folders rather than dumping them all into a common folder on your hard drive. The best time to do this is when transferring the photos from your camera to your computer. I recommend maintaining a master folder on a hard drive in which you keep all the digital photo folders.

Because I use the Organizer, this named folder division approach to organizing photos isn't mandatory because the software knows the names and locations of all the photos. Even though I am using Organizer, I still maintain the images in separate folders in case something catastrophic, like a virus attack, were to happen to the catalog file. In such a situation it would be difficult to reconstruct the grouping of the photos without a fundamental folder organization like the example shown in **Figure 5.1**.

Organization Workflow

I am not an organized person. My office stands in mute testimony to that fact. I would have included a photo to prove my point but the publisher said that we would have to include warning labels on the book. My lifetime motto is: If a cluttered desk is the sign of a cluttered mind, what is a clean and empty desk the sign of? I say all this so you don't think the following recommendations are the ravings of an obsessive, neat person and, therefore, probably won't work for you.

As we saw in Figure 5.1, I use nested folders (folders placed within folders) to further group my photos together. The example is not something I created to demonstrate a concept. It is actually part of my 65,000+ image library located on a very large hard drive. Here is how that particular organization came to be.

When I was in Washington, D.C. taking photos for three days, I took my notebook—of course—to capture and catalog all of the images I shot each day. Keep in mind that I probably shoot more photos in a day than most vacationers shoot in several weeks. On my notebook, I created three daily folders, one for each shooting day.

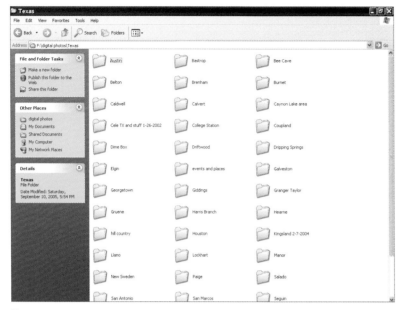

Figure 5.1
Organizing by event, place, or location serves as a good foundation for any image management plan.

Every evening I would sit in the motel room and do the following:

- Download the images from the camera into the daily folder.

- Review the photos using the Organizer, deleting the bad ones (there were many) and identifying particularly good ones.

- Add keywords to the photos using the Organizer.

- Back up the daily shooting onto a CD-ROM.

Move and Copy—What's the Difference?

When you are relocating folders, you may have two options—to Copy or to Move the folder. To Copy the folder means that a duplicate of the folder and its contents is created. To Move a folder means that the folder and its contents are duplicated and then the original is deleted. The operating system provides the Copy and Move commands. When using the Move command you should be aware that Windows verifies the copy that was made before deleting the original. Moving folders within one another in My Computer or Windows Explorer only requires that you drag one folder into another. If you want to move a file from one hard drive to another or one networked computer to another, you can right-click the folder you want to move and drag it to the destination. When you let go of the right mouse button a submenu pops up. The two top choices are, Copy Here and Move Here.

Upon returning home from my trip, I transferred all of the photos from my notebook computer to my main system and into a folder named Washington, D.C., keeping them organized in folders the way they were in my notebook (**Figure 5.2**).

When there were several folders for out-of-state locations, I created a U.S. folder and moved all of the folders that did not contain Texas (my home state) photos into it. Yes, I know Texas is part of the U.S.—in theory at least. For more information about moving and copying folders in Windows, see the sidebar, "Move and Copy—What's the Difference?"

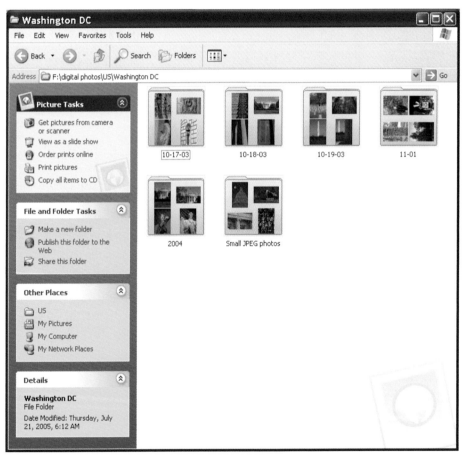

Figure 5.2
Folders in My Computer show content without creating catalogs.

Be Ready to Modify Your Changes

I shared my workflow with you so that you could understand that while my image file folder organization has become quite complex, it began as a simple system and grew as the collection grew.

Sometimes you will reorganize your folders and discover that it doesn't work as expected. When this happens, rearrange again. For example, I initially kept all my Texas photos in folders named after the cities in which they were shot. It wasn't long before there were several hundred folders under Texas—it's a big state. I tried several schemes until I came up with a sub-grouping that divided the state into major cities, and several folders for grouping together the hundreds of smaller towns like Oatmeal, Muleshoe, and of course Lukenbach.

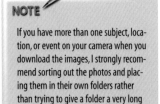

NOTE

If you have more than one subject, location, or event on your camera when you download the images, I strongly recommend sorting out the photos and placing them in their own folders rather than trying to give a folder a very long combination name, such as Billy Bob's wedding 2003/Wild Reception Party 2003/Divorce Proceeding 2004.

Folder Naming Suggestions

The easiest folder names are those named for an event (for example, Amanda's Wedding, Baby's First Birthday). Don't clutter the folder name with a date unless it's necessary; usually, just the month/year (Track Meet 3-04) is sufficient. Don't use long folder names or part of the name will get lost (**Figure 5.3**).

For photos not related to specific events, use location (Hawaii 2005) or subject matter (for example, Bluebonnets or Clouds).

Now that we've covered some image management fundamentals, let's learn how to use the tools in Elements to organize and manage your photos.

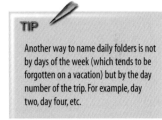

TIP

Another way to name daily folders is not by days of the week (which tends to be forgotten on a vacation) but by the day number of the trip. For example, day two, day four, etc.

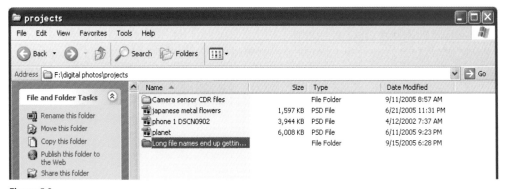

Figure 5.3
Avoid long folder names.

Using the Organizer

I want to repeat a few things here before we get started just in case you started reading the book on this page. Photoshop Elements is really two programs. It consists of the Editor and the Organizer. The Organizer is a separate program that, when launched, can run at the same time that the Editor is running. Both programs work seamlessly with one another, but remember, they are two separate programs.

You can use the Organizer to view just about any form of media that is available today. You can see all of your photos and video clips, and even store audio files. From the Photo Browser mode of the Organizer, you can download photos from your digital camera, photos from your scanner, a CD, and DVD, to name only a few sources. You can organize items into categories by attaching tags to the images, and you can also quickly move an image from the Photo Browser into the Editor with the click of a button.

How the Organizer Works

Probably the biggest speed bump for first-time users of the Organizer has to do with how the Organizer works as compared with how Windows' familiar My Computer interface works. When you open a folder using My Computer (**Figure 5.4**) you see what's in the folder (depending on the View option you have selected). You can jump into a folder, wait a few moments for Windows to create some thumbnails, and you're ready to rock.

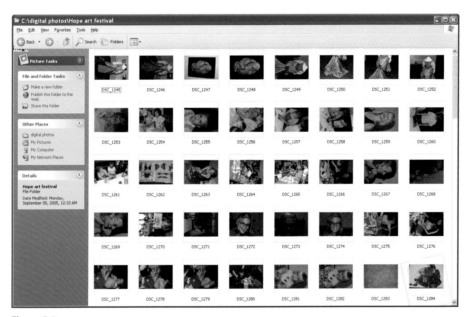

Figure 5.4
My Computer shows folder content without cataloging the images first.

The main limitation to using My Computer to manage your photos is that you need to know where (in which drive and in what folder) the desired image is stored. If your digital photo collection consists of a few folders like the one shown in **Figure 5.5**: *Our Dream Wedding 2000*, *Monster Truck Pulls 2000-2004*, and *My Divorce Party 2005*, you are always going to know where your favorite photo is located.

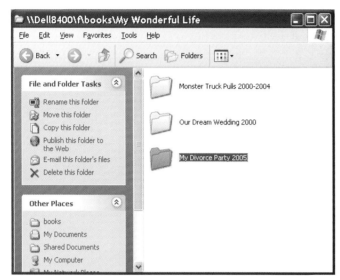

Figure 5.5
It is easy to find photos when you only have a few to keep track of.

As your tiny digital photo collection grows, it will soon consist of thousands of photos scattered over dozens of folders and on different disk drives. Locating a specific photo then becomes problematic, especially after you haven't worked with the photos in a few months and you no longer remember which folder contained the photo you wanted to send a friend.

If there is a downside to using the Organizer, it is that your photos need first to be cataloged before they can be viewed. So, the first time you open the Organizer you are facing a blank screen (**Figure 5.6**, next page).

If you have a large existing photo collection, it can take some time to catalog your entire collection. Once the photos are cataloged, you can view all the thumbnails in the same window regardless of where the files are located on your computer—or even off of your computer (more on that in a moment). My Computer allows you look at the contents of one folder at a time. With Organizer, you can use the thumbwheel of your mouse to smoothly scroll through your entire collection, or you can find photos based on the date they were taken, or you can assign keywords to them so that with a single click you can find all of the photos of your son or select just your vacation photos.

For those of you who still like to view images one folder at a time, Adobe has added a Folder Location view arrangement in the Photo Browser. When the Organizer is in this display arrangement (**Figure 5.7**) it displays the cataloged contents of the selected folder on the left—assuming that the contents have been cataloged.

That concludes the overview of how it works. Now let's take a quick tour of the Organizer workspace.

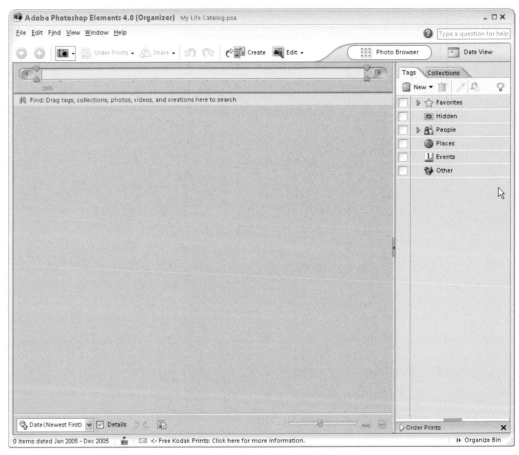

Figure 5.6
The first time you open the Organizer the main window is blank.

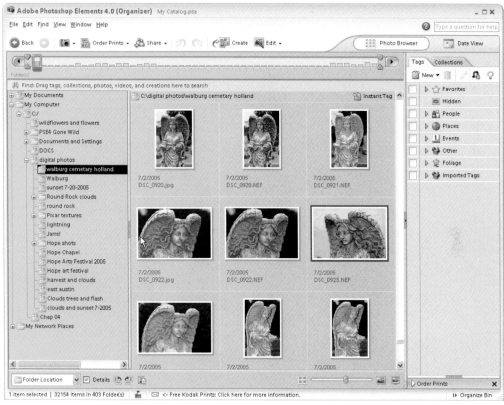

Figure 5.7
Folder Location is one of the four different ways photos can be arranged in the Photo Browser.

The Organizer Workspace

The Organizer has two modes of operation: the Photo Browser (**Figure 5.8**, next page) and the Date View (**Figure 5.9**, next page). You can do almost everything from the Photo Browser, while the Date View lets you see photos displayed in a calendar format, which shows the images by day, month, or even year. Because most of your daily work will involve using the Photo Browser mode, let's take a closer look at it.

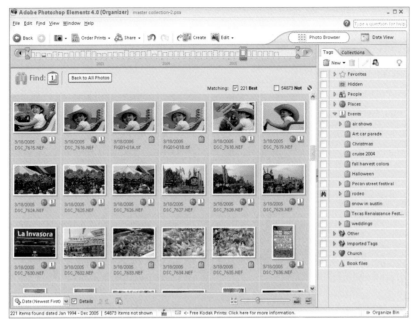

Figure 5.8
The Photo Browser is the Organizer mode you will use most often.

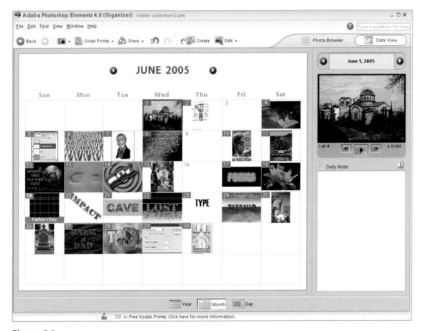

Figure 5.9
The Date View offers a quick view of your photos in a calendar-style format.

A Quick Tour of the Photo Browser

The Photo Browser is a workspace that is dense with buttons and menus to launch you into other applications. In this chapter we are going to focus our attention on the organizational tools.

There are several ways to open the Photo Browser. When you launch Photoshop Elements you can choose to go directly to the Organizer from the Welcome screen (**Figure 5.10**). From the Editor, just click the Photo Browser button in the shortcuts bar.

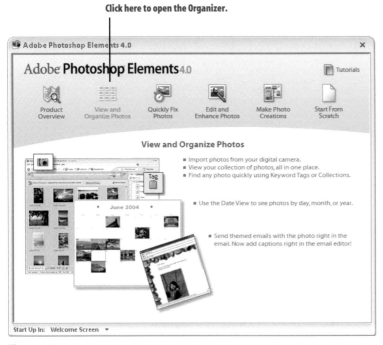

Figure 5.10
The opening Welcome screen is one way to get to the Photo Browser.

The following is a short list that describes the major components of the Photo Browser shown in **Figure 5.11** and gives a brief summary of what each one does. We'll learn more as we actually learn to use them.

- **Timeline**. Probably one of the most useful features in the Photo Browser, the timeline helps you find photos by dates along the timeline. You can toggle it on and off using Ctrl+L.

- **Date View**. You can switch the Organizer to Date View.

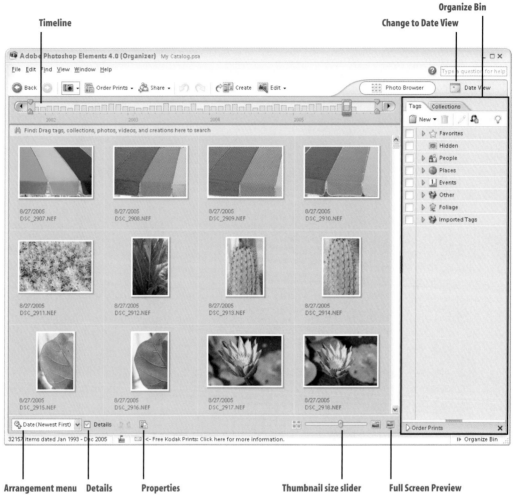

Figure 5.11
The Photo Browser interface of the Organizer.

- **Organize Bin**. All of the tags, categories, subcategories (like keywords), and collections appear in the Organize Bin.

- **Photo Browser Arrangement**. From here you can change the order of how thumbnails appear in the Photo Well. Their order of appearance can be according to date, when they were brought into Elements (import batch), or by the location of the folders containing the images.

- **Thumbnail size slider**. This controls the size of the thumbnails displayed in the Photo Browser.

- **Details**. The details option shows or hides the creation date, tags, and collections for items in the Photo Browser.

- **Image Properties**. When selected, the properties of any selected image, or images, appear on the lower-left side of the Photo Browser window.

- **Full Screen Preview**. Clicking this icon instantly produces a slide show for reviewing selected photos.

Putting the Photo Browser to Work

Since Adobe has included some excellent material in both the printed manual and the online help guide, I thought it best not to repeat what they have provided. Instead, let's concentrate on using the Photo Browser to organize and manage some photos by going through setting, organizing, and managing a typical photo catalog.

Creating a New Catalog

In Chapter 2 you learned how to move images to your computer. Now, we will learn how to move them into a catalog.

1. Open the Organizer either by selecting it from the Welcome screen or clicking the Organizer button above the Editor menu bar.

2. When in Organizer, make sure you are in the Photo Browser view. How your Browser appears depends on settings from the last time it was used, so don't be concerned if yours looks different than the sample in Figure 5.11.

3. Choose File, Catalog, and the dialog shown in **Figure 5.12** appears. Click the New button which opens a New Catalog dialog. Name the catalog "My Sample Catalog" and click OK. You now have a new blank catalog.

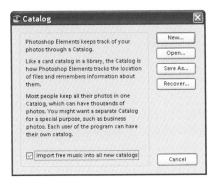

Figure 5.12
The Catalog dialog is where all catalog related actions are selected.

Filling the New Catalog with Images

When it is time to add photos to your catalog, here is how to do it:

1. Click on the Camera icon shown in **Figure 5.13** and select From Files and Folders (Ctrl+Shift+G).

2. When the Get Photos from Files and Folders dialog opens (**Figure 5.14**), change the source location to the file folder containing your photos. Select all of the files in the folder by using Ctrl+A. If the photos you are cataloging have many photos of people with red eye, click the Automatically Fix Red Eyes check box. If there are only a few such photos, don't use this feature because it greatly slows cataloging while Elements examines each photo for red eye.

3. When all the photos are selected, click the Get Photos button and after a few moments, you have a new catalog of images (**Figure 5.15**). A message box appears stating "The only items in the main window are those you just imported. To see the rest of the catalog, click Back to All Photos." Click OK.

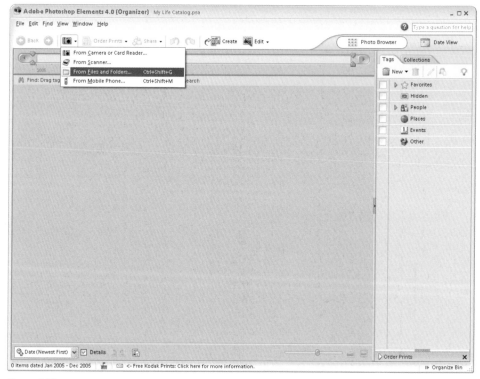

Figure 5.13
Cataloging existing photos begins here.

Figure 5.14
Select the photos that you want
cataloged.

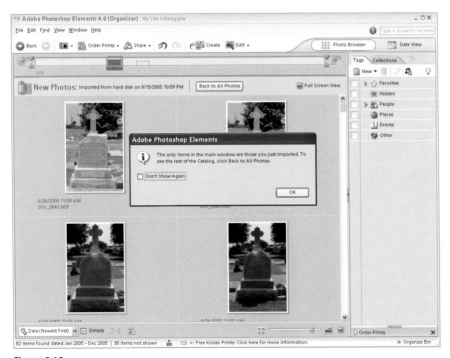

Figure 5.15
When cataloging is finished only the newly cataloged images appear.

Working with Tags

Before we begin tagging images, you need to understand a few points about how they work. Tags are like keywords that you can attach to your images. Adding a tag doesn't alter the image to which it is attached, it just adds information that allows the Organizer to find and organize the images.

Keywords are descriptive words or phrases used to identify subjects or component parts of an image. In the Organizer, keywords are called Tags, Categories, or Subcategories. The success of organizing your collection is determined, in part, by your choice of keywords (or tags).

It is important to know that the Photo Browser doesn't move images around, but rather, keeps track of the photos right where they are. With the Organizer, every time you get photos from a location that is on or attached to your computer, the Photo Browser makes a note where those files are located. Even though the thumbnails appear together in the main window, they may actually be scattered throughout your system.

For example, after getting several hundred files from many different folders into a catalog, I create a tag called "Grace" and then attach it to every thumbnail that includes my daughter Grace. Later, by putting a check by her tag in the Organize Bin, all photos with that tag, regardless of where the photos are stored on my system, appear in the main window.

You can attach more than one tag to an item. For instance, you might have tags with the names of individual people, subject matter, locations, and events that you have photographed. By attaching multiple tags to your photos, you could search for these tags to make searches even more accurate. A recent example of this was when I was taking some photos of a hot air balloon race at Houston's NASA Space Center. While I was there, I took some great photos of a rocket they were refurbishing. I have taken many photos at NASA, so if I wanted to find those photos, I would select the NASA tag and the hot air balloon event tag. Only the NASA photos I took during that shoot would be displayed in the main window.

Types of Tags

Everything having to do with tags is done in the Organize Bin of the Photo Browser. When you created the new catalog, you may have noticed that there are, by default, four categories of tags in the Organize Bin. They are the following:

- People
- Places
- Events
- Other

You aren't limited to using just these four general categories by any means. You can create your own categories and multiple levels of subcategories as well. In addition to the default tags and any that you create, there are two special classifications of tags:

- **Favorites**. This category is my personal favorite (no pun intended). This is how you identify your really great photos (I call these keepers) and later you can find them by choosing what level of quality you have tagged them with. The Favorites contains tags with 1 to 5 stars indicated (**Figure 5.16**). An image can have only one favorite tag attached. After all, if you tagged an image as being a 5-star favorite, putting a 2-star favorite tag would be confusing at best.

- **Hidden**. Items with a Hidden tag attached don't appear in the Photo Browser unless the Hidden tag is included as one of the search criteria. So if you mark a file with both a Most Embarrassing Moments and a Hidden tag, those holiday photos won't appear when the Most Embarrassing Moments tag is selected as long as the Hidden tag isn't selected.

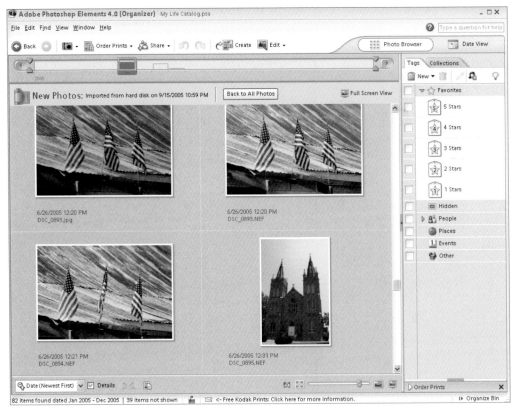

Figure 5.16
The Favorite tag allows you to keep track of your best work.

Creating New Tags

The default set of tags isn't adequate to catalog anything. To create a catalog that meets your needs requires creating your own set of tags, which is quite easy to do. Here is how it is done:

1. With the Organize Bin selected, click the New button from the toolbar, and choose New Tag from the drop-down menu (**Figure 5.17**).

2. When the Create Tag dialog appears choose Category, then select the category from the drop-down list.

3. In the Name text window, name the tag, and click OK. The new tag appears in the Organize Bin under the selected category (**Figure 5.18**). The icon for the new tag is a question mark and it will remain so until it is attached to its first photo.

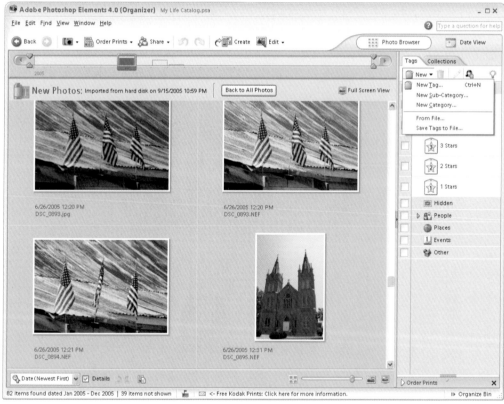

Figure 5.17
Creating a New Tag.

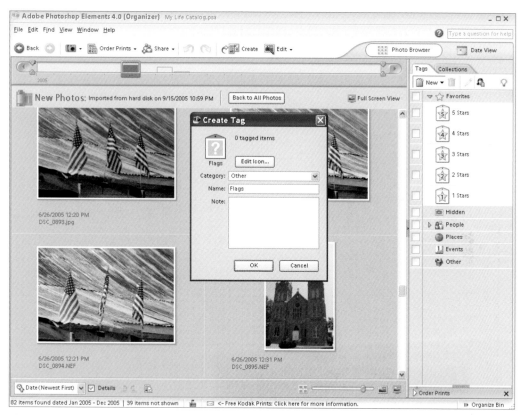

Figure 5.18
The New Tag dialog offers several organizational options.

Choosing the Name for a Tag

When adding a keyword, ask yourself this question: Will I ever search for this photo using this keyword? For **Figure 5.19**, I assigned the following tags:

- **University of Tampa, Tampa.** Location is usually a strong keyword. In this case, the minarets are unique to Tampa and its university. If I wanted to find this photo I would first search using the keyword *Tampa*, which would give me a lot of hits, but it would include all of the minaret photos.

- **Minaret.** This might seem to be the best choice, but I probably wouldn't search on it. Why? Because minaret is not a common word to me and it's possible that I spelled it wrong when the keyword was added (Elements doesn't offer a spell checker—that's a hint, Adobe). I would first search on the location, even though it would produce many more hits that must be searched through, to find the minaret photos.

- **Architecture, Detail.** I use these two keywords a lot. Any photo of a building that is not a barn (remember, I live in Texas) is assigned this keyword. The keyword detail means it was a close-up shot of a portion of the subject.

- **Crescent Moon.** This is one of those once-in-a-blue-moon keywords you add that might cause the photo to turn up when you least expect it, but, need to use for a specific project.

Shakespeare said "Brevity is the soul of wit," and in like manner, the same can be said for the assignment of keywords. Only include those keywords absolutely necessary to group or locate a photo. In the previous example (Figure 5.19), the other possibilities that were not included were:

- **Moroccan.** The style of the hotel (it originally was built as a hotel) was Moroccan.

- **Plant.** The name of the building is Plant Hall.

- **Aluminum.** The minaret is constructed using aluminum.

- **Sky.** Yes, there is a sky but in this case it is just a blue backgrond.

- **Pole.** That's what is under the crescent moon.

Figure 5.19
Inspiration for many good, and bad, tags.

Bottom line, only assign essential keywords that will help you—not others—find a photo later on.

Now let's learn how to add keywords using the Organizer.

Attaching a Tag to a Single Photo

Once you have made a new tag, here is how simple it is to assign it to a photo.

- Click and drag the new tag you just created from the Organize Bin onto the thumbnail of the photo you want to tag. The question mark icon in the new tag is replaced with a tiny thumbnail of the photo and a small icon appears in the lower-right corner of the thumbnail. The icon that appears is the one that is assigned to the Places tag. If you place the cursor over the icon in the thumbnail's left-hand corner, the name of the attached tag appears (**Figure 5.20**).

Tag icon

Figure 5.20
An icon in the corner of the thumbnail area indicates that the photo has a tag assigned to it.

Attaching Tags to Multiple Photos

You can attach the same tag to multiple photos using the following technique:

1. Select all the photos in the main window that you want to attach the tag to. Use Ctrl+click to select multiple photos. Each selected photo is highlighted with a blue border.

2. Click and drag the tag on top of any of the selected thumbnails in the main window. When you release the mouse button, the tag is applied to all of the selected photos (**Figure 5.21**).

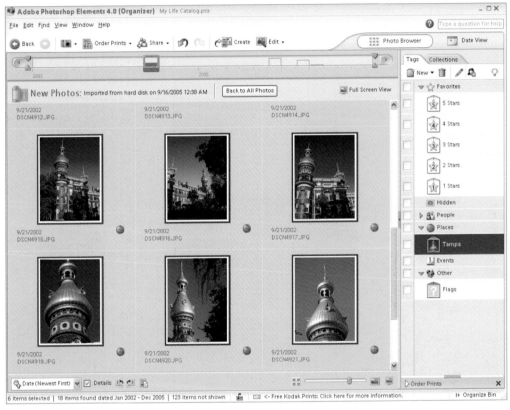

Figure 5.21
A single tag can be applied to multiple photos.

Finding Photos Using Tags

Now that you have some of the photos tagged, let's use the tags to find the photos we want. Like everything else in Elements, there is more than one way to use tags to search for photos, but the following are the fastest and best ways to do it.

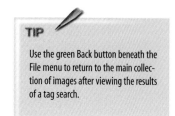

TIP

Use the green Back button beneath the File menu to return to the main collection of images after viewing the results of a tag search.

In the Organize Bin, double-click the tag of the photos that you want to find. All the photos with that tag attached will appear in the main window (**Figure 5.22**).

Another way to search for photos using a tag is to click the blank box to the left of the tag name. A binoculars icon appears and all of the photos that have this tag attached appear in the main window.

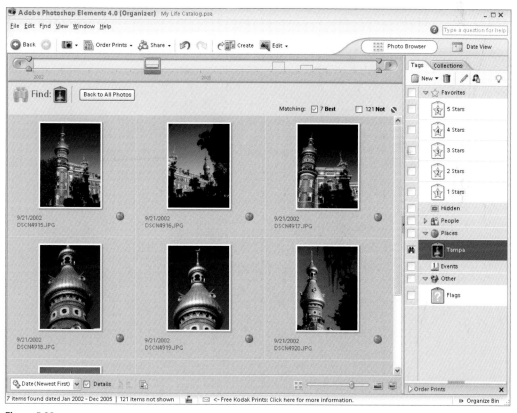

Figure 5.22
Double-click any tag in the Organize Bin to see all the photos tagged with that tag.

Multiple Tag Searches

You can find photos with multiple tags by clicking the blank box next to all the tags that you want to use as search criteria. Elements will include all the photos that match any of the tags selected. When searching, a large number of photos could produce a lot of close matches with one but not all of the tags. The Photo Browser lists the results in a way to help you narrow the search.

Changing Tags

As you create additional tags, you need to move folders into others to prevent the list of tags from becoming so long as to be unmanageable. Changing the hierarchy of tags in the Organize Bin is really easy. Here is how to do it:

NOTE

If you want to move a subcategory tag from one folder to another you only need to drag the tag from one Tag folder to another.

- Right-click on one of your photo tags and select Change the tag to a sub-category. You can tell that the tag has become a sub-category when it no longer has a thumbnail.

Using File Info to Add More Information

You can use the File Info feature of Photoshop Elements to input additional information about the photograph. With an image open, select File, File Info to open a dialog that provides five selectable pages for information (**Figure 5.23**). The Description page displays a wealth of information (that you must add) including copyright, title, comments, and so on. If you choose to make the image copyrighted, a copyright symbol appears in the title bar whenever the image is opened.

The remaining pages in File Info are mostly read-only data. The two Camera Data pages provide a lot of technical information about the image that was provided by the camera when the image was shot (**Figure 5.24**). Sometimes, these pages are blank because the information was either not recorded by the camera, the image was scanned, or (something that's quite common) the data was lost when the file was copied by an application that doesn't preserve the image data.

Working with Collections

The Photo Browser offers an additional way to rearrange your photos to create slide shows or bound books called Creations. When creating a slide show using tagged photos, you must accept the order in which they appear while a Collection allows you to rearrange photos to any order.

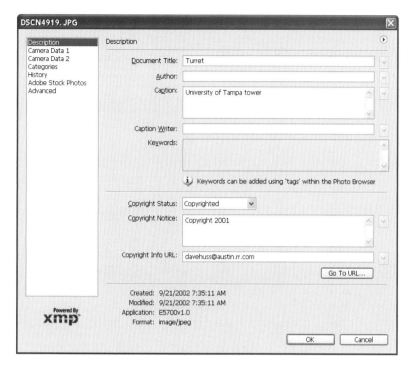

Figure 5.23
File Info box contains both camera-generated data and data that you add.

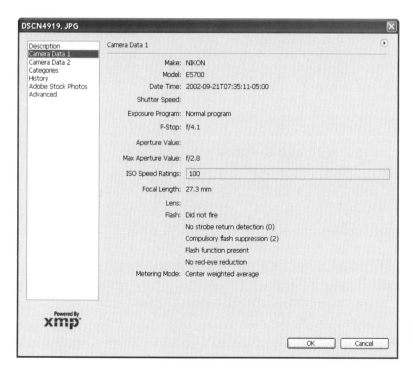

Figure 5.24
This box contains a wealth of camera settings data.

Catalog Maintenance

Now you have your image catalog put together and all of your photos are identified with tags. Most of the time you don't need to be concerned about your catalogs, but making regular backups of them is essential for protecting your photos in case something happens to your catalogs. This section covers some basic procedures to back up and maintain your image catalogs.

Face Tagging

A feature that is new in Photoshop Elements 4, is called Face Tagging. This is a cool feature that searches through all of the photos that you select and detects all of the faces and shows them as little thumbnails as shown in **Figure 5.25**. So, what would you do with this? During testing, I found Face Tagging was really handy since I take a lot of photos of people in groups. In one case, I needed a photo that had a specific person in it. Running the Face Tagging (Find, Find Faces for Tagging) produced a list like the one shown in Figure 5.25 from which it was relatively easy to find the person I was looking for. From this display you can assign tags for specific groups of people, like family, in-laws, outlaws, etc. The Face Tagging feature is surprisingly accurate as well. In a recent test of 398 images that the feature tagged, only two were not human faces. While this feature could stand some tweaking (for speed), overall it is pretty cool.

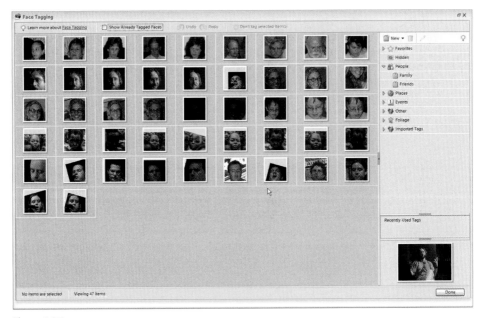

Figure 5.25
Many similar photos take up space in the main window.

Stacks and Versions

Stacks and Versions are my favorite features and yet most users don't know they are even there. Stacks are for those situations when you have many photos of the same subject, which is the norm when it comes to taking photos of a model or a product. Rather than display them all separately as shown in **Figure 5.26** where the girl is featured, you can combine them all into a single image as shown in the upper-right stacked photo in **Figure 5.27**, next page. All of the images are there, they are just hidden under the master images.

Versions is another boon to anyone who works on photos. Before the Organizer, when you wanted to save a variation of a photo, you had to save the image with names like London_01, London_02, London_03. Versions maintains many versions of the image in a single address spaces and you can easily break out the individual photos. Both Stacks and Version have been greatly improved in this latest release.

Figure 5.26
Here the tagged photos are displayed separately.

Figure 5.27
Using the Stack feature allows the photos to be stacked in a single thumbnail.

Backing up Catalogs

Depending on how big your catalog is, backing it up can take a long time. So, when you open your catalog and see the reminder message asking if you want to back up your catalog now, most likely you don't want to do it right at that time. Here is how to do it when you do have the time:

1. Choose File, Backup. The Burn/Backup dialog opens and the Backup the Catalog option should already be selected (**Figure 5.28**). Click Next.

2. The Backup Options of the Burn/Backup dialog appears next. If this is the first backup you have done, you need to select Full Backup. Incremental Backup only copies files created or changed since the last backup.

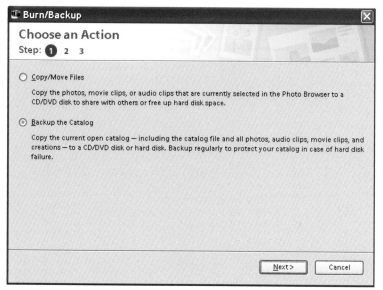

Figure 5.28
The Recover feature can quickly restore damaged catalogs.

3. The last dialog allows you to select the output device or path. If you select a CD or DVD recorder (burner), the very first time you use it, Photo Browser will first run some data timing tests before backing up your images. If you are backing up to CD or DVD, and it requires more space than is available on the disc, the backup will pause, and you will be prompted for additional discs.

Moving Photos off of Your Computer

Just because something appears in a catalog in the Organizer doesn't mean it has to be taking up space on your hard drive. The Organizer has the ability to let you move those photos that have sentimental value, like your second cousin's graduation from the fifth grade (after only two attempts), to an archive CD or DVD. The thumbnails still appear in the catalog but if you actually need to access them, it will ask you to insert the specific disc.

The backup feature is a little weak, to be honest, since there is much better backup built into the XP operating system, but there is one great aspect to it. It nags you to back up your images when you reopen the collection and have added images since the last backup. This is critical

> **NOTE**
>
> If any files in your catalog have been moved, it doesn't mean that they're lost, only that the catalog has lost track of their location. The most common cause of this problem is when the images are moved to a different location. Most of the time, Elements can find the missing files pretty quickly. If the files aren't found automatically, the Missing Files Check Before Backup dialog opens and you can then point Photo Browser to where the files have moved. If the files the catalog is looking for are actually gone, click the Remove from Catalog button and Photo Browser will purge any references to the missing image files from the catalog. Once you have located missing files, you can continue making a backup.

because hard drives are the component most likely to fail in a computer. If you have several years worth of photos on a hard drive and no backup, it may only cost you a few hundred dollars to replace the hard drive, but you can never replace the photos. Back up your photos regularly and keep the CDs or DVDs on which they are stored in a safe place, preferably at a remote location from your computer.

In the previous section you learned how the catalog can locate files that were inadvertently moved. So what do you do when you want to move older images off of the computer to make room for new photos? The Photo Browser has the option of copying or moving these files to a CD-ROM or DVD, using the Burn command. The advantage of using the Burn command is that the catalog knows where the files were moved to. The thumbnails remain in the catalog and if you select a photo that has been moved off of the computer, you will be prompted to insert the CD/DVD containing the requested file. Here is the procedure to move files off of your system.

1. Open the images that you want to copy or move in the Photo Browser.

2. Choose File, Burn (Ctrl+B), and the dialog that appears is the same as that which appears when selecting a backup, except that the option Copy/Move Files is selected.

3. The next dialog features options to specify how files are to be moved offline and deleted from the original source.

Recovering and Restoring Catalogs

So you're importing some photos into an existing catalog and your computer crashes. When you restart the computer and Photo Browser, you discover that the catalog you were importing the photo into is corrupted. If your catalog ever becomes corrupted, there is a tool in Photo Browser to recover it.

1. Choose File, Catalog, and then click the Recover button. The Recover/Catalog dialog opens.

2. Click OK and Photo Browser repairs damaged catalogs.

The Organizer and the Photo Browser are much improved in Elements and there is a good deal more to them. To see what else these programs can do, take some time and review what Adobe included in the online help files.

In the next chapter, we will learn how to do even more cool stuff with Elements.

6 Dazzling Effects and Professional Techniques

This chapter is a collection of things you can do using Photoshop Elements. It includes emphasizing a subject by creating a false depth of field, creating a hand-tinted look to your favorite photos, and isolating color for effect. You will also discover the fun of converting photos into puzzles.

Emphasizing the Subject

Oftentimes when you take a photograph of someone or something, the subject gets lost in the background or the background is too close, like the stone wall in the wedding photo shown in **Figure 6.1**.

Figure 6.1
A cluttered background is distracting.

The secret to emphasizing the subject isn't done by eliminating the background, it is accomplished by creating a false sense of depth of field (DOF). If you're not familiar with the term, see the sidebar "Understanding Depth of Field." The typically wide-angle lenses of digital cameras tend to produce a wide depth of field and, as a result, the background is often in sharp focus. It is therefore necessary to use Elements to blur the background as it would appear had the camera produced it.

Later in this chapter you will learn how to make the background in Figure 6.1 slightly out of focus to emphasize the subject. The procedure involves isolating the background with a selection, and then blurring it. There are many ways to isolate the background and the exercise will show you how to use the Magnetic Lasso and Polygonal Lasso tools in combination to quickly select the background. First, however, it's important to explain how selections work.

Understanding Depth of Field

Depth of field is an optical phenomenon produced by the camera lens. When a lens focuses on a subject at a distance, all subjects at that distance are in focus while subjects that are not at the same distance (that are either closer or farther away) appear out of focus. The zone in which the subject is in focus is referred to as the depth of field (DOF). If you are unfamiliar with photography, here is some useful information. The amount of DOF is controlled by the size of the aperture (f-stop), which, along with the shutter speed, is automatically set by your camera when shooting. If you are shooting pictures when there's a lot of light, the lens aperture is set to a small opening (large f-stop number) and the resulting DOF is at its greatest, meaning that almost everything is in focus. When there is low lighting, the aperture is opened to its largest size (smallest f-stop) and only the subject and very little else is in focus.

Understanding Selections

Photoshop Elements has a large number of different tools whose only purpose is to define the part of the image where we want to work. The defined area is called a selection. All the tools used to make the selections are known as selection tools, with names such as Magnetic Lasso and Magic Wand. If this is your first time using Photoshop Elements, don't let the large number of selection tools and their strange-sounding names overwhelm you. We introduce them one step at a time, beginning with a look at what a selection actually is.

In theory, we all have used selections at one time or another and I've heard many analogies to them. Here are a few: If you have ever used a stencil, you have used a selection. The stencil allows you to apply paint to part of the material while keeping the rest of the material from being coated in paint. Another example of a selection that's closer to home (literally) is the use of masking tape to mask off parts of a room on which you don't want to get paint—which, for me, would be the whole room. Selections in Photoshop Elements act just like a stencil or masking tape when it comes to applying any effect to an image: one part of your image can be altered while keeping another part intact. Let's look at the most basic of the selection tools: the Marquee tools.

Introducing the Marquee Tools

The Marquee tools appear near the top of the Toolbox (**Figure 6.2**). They can be used to create selections in the shapes of rectangles and ellipses. If you access the Options bar, you can also create unique selections in fixed shapes.

If this is your first time working with Elements, the Marquee tools might seem to be limited. After all, how often will you need to select a square, rectangle, ellipsis, or circle? In fact, you can create about any shape imaginable using these tools if you learn how to use some of the features found in the Options bar (**Figure 6.3**).

Using Marquee Tools: Some Tips and Tricks

There are several keyboard combinations that will be helpful as you work with the Marquee tools

- Shift key—When pressed after the mouse is clicked, the Shift key forces (constrains) the Ellipse tool to a circle and the Rectangle marquee to a square. If you don't do this, it is nearly impossible to get a square- or a circle-shaped selection.

- Alt key—Pressing this key after clicking the mouse makes the marquee produced by the tool expand outward from the center. If you didn't have this option, it could take forever to get the selection centered.

Figure 6.2
The Marquee tools are the basic building blocks for many selections.

Figure 6.3
Using the Elliptical Marquee tool (and a few other Elements tricks), this simple sunflower is transformed into something radically different.

Rounding Up the Lasso Tools

The Lasso tools, which are located under the Marquee tools in the Toolbox, are a collection of three different tools that you can use to draw both straight-edged and freehand edges when making an irregularly-shaped selection. The three tools are the Lasso tool, Polygonal Lasso tool, and Magnetic Lasso tool.

Unlike the Marquee tools, which produce closed shapes, the Lasso tools let you draw a meandering path around a subject and, when you are done, you can either let go of the mouse or double-click it (this depends on the tool you are using) and Photoshop Elements will make a straight line back to the starting point to complete the selection.

All these tools act in a similar fashion. In the grand scheme of things, the Lasso tool is designed to draw freehand selections and the Polygonal Lasso tool is excellent for making selections that require straight lines. The Magnetic Lasso tool is similar to its two Lasso-tool cousins, except it has the capability to automatically cling to the edges of contrast objects, which can save you so much work. If you hold the Alt key, it becomes a freehand tool just like the Lasso tool.

Controlling the Magnetic Lasso

The Magnetic Lasso tool is a great timesaver when it comes to making selections. Essentially, as you move the tool along an edge that you want to select, the tool is constantly looking for and creating a selection along the edge. On a high contrast, well-defined edge, it works better than advertised. On edges that are poorly defined, in that the colors inside and outside the edge are very near the same color, it needs some help from you.

Using the tool is relatively simple. Click once on the point where you want to begin the selection. This point is called a fastening point. Now, move the tool (slowly and without holding the mouse button) along the edge. Fastening points appear along the edge of the selection as the computer tries to automatically determine where the edge is. At some point, the computer will guess wrong. When it does, stop and press the backspace key. Each time you press this key, Photoshop removes the last point on the selection. Continue to do this until you get to a point on the selection that is on the actual edge. You can try it again, but usually, when the Magnetic tool is guessing wrong, there's either a low-contrast edge or there is something nearby (not on the edge) that is pulling the tool away from the edge.

At this point, you have several choices. You can change the settings in the Options bar, click your way through it (I'll explain in a moment), or temporarily change Lasso tools. I rarely recommend changing the options settings. So, here is what I recommend you try. When you hit a rough patch, if the edge is irregular (lots of ins and outs), you can click each of the points that define the edge, which puts them closely together. Another option is to temporarily switch to the Lasso tool by holding the Alt key and dragging the mouse along the edge with the mouse button depressed. In images where the subject being selected is close to the color of the background so that it blends with the shadows or background, the Magnetic Lasso tool might not be the best tool to use. To get a good selection, the Magnetic Lasso tool needs a fairly distinctive edge with which to work.

Getting the Best Selections (In the Least Amount of Time)

Whether doing art layout for work or for community projects (read: free), I have spent the past ten years making selections and the resulting composite images. In that time, I developed a short list of "do's" and "dont's" that I'll share with you to help you make great selections.

- **Do Make a First Rough Cut Selection**

  If the image is large enough so that it does not fit on the screen when you view it at 100% (Actual Pixels setting), shift the zoom level to Fit On Screen by either pressing Ctrl+0 (zero) or double-clicking the Zoom or Hand tools in the Toolbox and making a rough selection. It doesn't matter which selection tool you use. You just want to get as close as you can without spending too much time doing it. This selection gets you in the ballpark.

- **Zoom and Move**

  Set the Zoom to Actual Pixels. Use either Ctrl+0 (zero) or double-click the Zoom or Hand tools in the Toolbox. I know, the image no longer fits on the screen, but it doesn't matter. There are several ways to move around when you're this close, but the best way I know of is to press the spacebar so that your currently selected tool becomes the Hand tool (as long as you keep the spacebar depressed). This is a lifesaver when you are drawing a selection and you find that you have come to the edge of the part displayed on the screen. When that happens, press the spacebar, drag the image to expose more of the subject on the screen, and when you let go of the spacebar, you return to your selection just where you left it.

- **Adding Some and Taking Some**

  Using the Add To Selection and Subtract From Selection modes begin to shape the selection to fit the subject you are trying to isolate. Here is a trick that saves time when doing this. First, instead of clicking the buttons in the Options bar, use the key modifiers to change between modes. Pressing the Shift key changes the selection mode to Add To and pressing the Alt key changes it to Subtract From. Just remember that these modifier keys must be pressed before you click the mouse. Second, in the Options bar, pick Add To as a mode so you need only to use the modifier key when you want to subtract from the selection.

- **Get in Close**

  On some areas, you might need to zoom in at levels even greater than 100% (Photoshop goes up to 1,600%, which allows you to select microbes and stray electrons.) Now and again, you must return to Fit To Screen just to keep a perspective on this entire image. Speaking of keeping a perspective, while you are improving the selection keep in mind the ultimate destination for the image you are selecting. Here are some examples of factors that should affect the degree of exactness you want to invest in your selection:

  - How close are the background colors of the image you are selecting and the current background colors? If they are roughly the same colors, investing a lot of time producing a detailed selection doesn't make much sense because a feathered edge works just fine.

  - Will the final image be larger, smaller, or the same size? If you are going to be making the current image larger, every detail will stick out like a sore thumb. So, any extra time you spend to make the selection as exact as possible will pay off big. If you are reducing the size of the subject, many tiny details will become lost when it's resized, so again, don't invest too much time in the selection.

  - Is this a paid job or a freebie? Creating a complex selection is a time-consuming process. I once spent nearly half a day on a single selection.

Creating a Depth of Field Focus Effect

As mentioned earlier, you can use the selection tools to isolate the background in your photograph. You then blur that background to emphasize your subject and create a false sense of depth of field.

Before starting with this exercise, it will help if you understand how to switch between the different lasso tools while you are making the selection. With the Magnetic Lasso tool selected, you can switch between the other Lasso tools:

- To switch to the Lasso tool, hold down the Alt key while moving the tool.

- To switch to the Polygonal Lasso tool, Alt-click the tool and it remains a Polygonal Lasso tool until the next time you click.

The following exercise uses the file **Wedding_couple.psd** which can be downloaded from the Peachpit Press Web site.

1. Open the file **Wedding_couple.psd**.

2. Choose the Magnetic Lasso tool in the Toolbox. In the Options bar, simply use the default settings of the tool. Click at the spot on the wall very near the groom's head as shown in **Figure 6.4** and move the tool along the edge of the subject's hair, creating a partial selection as you move to the bottom edge of the photograph. As you move the tool along the edge of the groom the tool creates a selection that follows the edge. If the tool selects the wrong edge, press the Delete key to erase a segment.

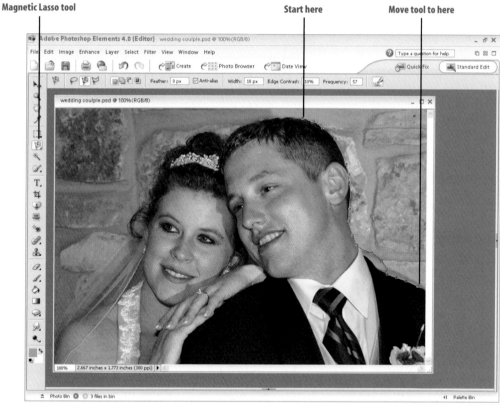

Figure 6.4
Select the area to be preserved using the Magnetic Lasso tool.

3. Now with the groom selected, we select the interior of the background edges with the Polygonal Lasso tool next. Hold down the Alt key and click where shown in **Figure 6.5**, near the shoulder of the groom. Release the Alt key and move the cursor to the upper-right corner of the photo (a straight line forms from the shoulder to this point). Complete this selection segment by clicking the left mouse button at a point in the upper-right corner. That last click also caused the tool to revert to a Magnetic Lasso. Alt-click again on the same point and the tool becomes a Polygonal tool again. Continue moving around the outer edge of the photo with this method until you get to the bottom-left corner.

4. When you reach the bottom-left corner, don't use the Alt key and carefully move the Magnetic Lasso tool along the edge of the bride, moving toward the starting point. To complete the selection, Ctrl+click the starting point and the selection is completed (**Figure 6.6**).

5. Now to make the background appear slightly out of focus. Choose Filter, Blur, Gaussian Blur. Change the blur setting to a radius of 6 pixels Click OK to apply the blur. Ctrl+D will deselect the bride and groom. (**Figure 6.7**).

This technique of creating a blurred background is quick and effective. The only drawback is that it permanently alters the photo. So let's look at another way of doing it.

Figure 6.5
Switch between different lasso tools to make the selection.

Figure 6.6
The completed selection.

Figure 6.7
Blurring the background emphasizes the subject.

How to Make and Use a Layer Mask

The problem with the technique we just looked at is that the background is permanently blurred. If at a later time you decide you want to see the background, you must locate the original and start all over again. Here is a technique that takes a little longer to create a softer background but produces no change to the original image and allows you to alter it at a later time.

The technique involves using a Layer mask, which is a familiar tool to Photoshop users. The challenge facing Elements users is that Adobe didn't include the Layer mask function. The good news is that with a few extra steps we can make our own Layer mask.

You will need to download the file **Longhorn.psd** from the Peachpit Press Web site. This longhorn steer (**Figure 6.8**) is enjoying a bite to eat (and in case you're wondering, the horns are real). The subject is on the left third of the photo, making for a good composition, but the overall background is distracting (not to him) so we need to soften it. Here is how it's done.

Figure 6.8
A great shot of a longhorn steer would look better if the barbed wire fence were removed.

1. Open the image **longhorn.psd**.

2. In the Layers palette make a copy of the background by clicking on the Background layer and dragging it on to the New Layer icon (**Figure 6.9**, next page).

3. With the background copy still selected, choose Gaussian Blur (Filter, Blur, Gaussian Blur). When the dialog opens, move the slider until the Radius is 4 pixels. Click OK (**Figure 6.10**, next page). The entire photo appears blurry.

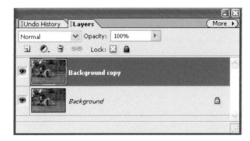

Figure 6.9
First, make a copy of the background.

Figure 6.10
Apply a Gaussian Blur to the background copy.

4. In the Layers palette select the Background layer. In the Menu choose Layer, New Adjustment Layer…Levels. When the dialog opens, name the layer the following: Layer Mask. This isn't necessary but it is a good habit to give descriptive names so you will remember when you see the layer a year from now. Click OK. When the Levels dialog appears, click OK without making any changes. Your Layers palette should look like **Figure 6.11**.

Figure 6.11
Add an Adjustment layer,
which will act as a Layer mask.

5. Select the top layer by clicking on it in the Layers palette Now comes the fun part. Choose Layer, Group with Previous (Ctrl+G). The layer's thumbnail has a small icon that appears to its left, indicating that this layer is linked to the layer below it (**Figure 6.12**).

Figure 6.12
Now the layers are linked, as
you can see by the icon that
appears.

6. To demonstrate the flexibility of the Layer mask, click on the Layer mask thumbnail in the Layers palette to select it. Select the Brush tool (B) and with the foreground color set to black, place the cursor on the image and paint over part of the foreground as shown in **Figure 6.13**, next page. The blurring disappears where you paint. A dark spot appears in the Layer mask thumbnail (within the Layers palette) in the area of the photo where you painted with the Brush tool.

7. To restore an area, all you need do is make the foreground color white (press the X key to eXchange the colors) and paint over the same area. The blurring of the top layer is once again visible. The final image is shown in **Figure 6.14**, next page.

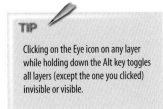

TIP

Clicking on the Eye icon on any layer while holding down the Alt key toggles all layers (except the one you clicked) invisible or visible.

TIP

If you click on the Layer mask thumbnail while holding down the Alt key, the clipping mask replaces the image in your workspace.

Figure 6.13
Paint out the blurred layer.

Figure 6.14
The finished photo.

Recapping the Layer Mask Exercise

Here is a summary of what you did in the Layer mask exercise and how it worked. We made a copy of the Background layer, selected the background and added an Adjustment layer (any of the Adjustment layers will work because we are using them as Layer masks), and finally grouped the top layer to the Adjustment layer.

NOTE

The actual mask in the Adjustment layer is technically called a clipping mask. The Adjustment layer, together with its clipping mask, operates as a Layer mask. I only mention this because you may come across the term clipping mask in some of the Elements online help files and user guide.

When the Group with Previous command is applied to the top layer, its visibility becomes controlled by the mask area of the Adjustment layer.

Everywhere on the mask that is black, the blurred layer on top becomes invisible. Everywhere it is white, the blurred layer is seen.

Because you can paint directly on the mask area you can control what parts appear blurred and what parts don't. Here is how to do that:

TIP

A quick way to evoke the Group with Previous command in the Layers palette is to place the cursor on the line separating the top layer and the Adjustment layer while holding down the Alt key. The cursor turns into a strange black ball and when it does, click on the line. The top layer is now linked to the Adjustment layer.

- To make part of the top layer visible, select the mask area in the Layers palette (Mask layer thumbnail) by clicking on it. Select the Brush tool and paint on the image using black. As you paint, the tiny thumbnail reflects the parts of the image that you have painted.

- To make part of the top layer invisible, do the same thing except use white.

- To make part of the top layer semi-transparent (which shows the background layer below), change the brush color to shades of gray.

Finishing Up the Job

The image now has several layers. To preserve the image so that you can make more changes at a later date, save the image as a Photoshop (PSD) or Tagged Image File Format (TIFF). To save in another format that can be used to send to friends, you must first flatten the image (Layer, Flatten Image) and then save it in any format you desire. Now that you know how to isolate and blur a background let's learn how to remove a background.

Replacing a Background

Professional portrait photographers almost always use a backdrop behind the subjects they are photographing. When taking photos at family gatherings or other events there isn't the opportunity (or the desire) to place a studio backdrop behind the subject so it must be done in Photoshop Elements.

In the past, removing a background was a cumbersome process but a new tool in Elements 4 makes the process relatively painless. Called the Magic Extractor, this tool can remove backgrounds quickly and cleanly—in most cases.

Using the Magic Extractor

The operation of the Magic Extractor is simple yet complex (that sounds so Zen). Before doing this next exercise let's review the Magic Extractor dialog (**Figure 6.15**), including the layout and operation of its tools.

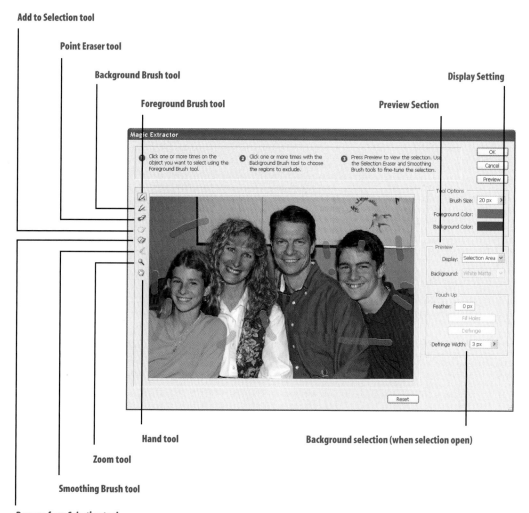

Figure 6.15
The Magic Extractor dialog.

Touch Up settings

The Magic Extractor produces selections based on the appearance of foreground and background areas that are marked when you use either the Foreground or Background Brush tool. After you mark the areas, click the Preview button and evaluate the results. Unless you are working with a polygonal subject against a white background you will need to make some adjustments. Use the Foreground and Background Brush tools to add and subtract from the background and check the results again with the Preview button. Finally, when the background is selected, apply the Magic Extractor by clicking the OK button. Only the foreground area appears in the photo when the image reappears in the Editor workspace.

Magic Extractor Workflow and Tips

Here are my suggestions for a workflow and for getting the most out of the Magic Extractor.

Use a minimum amount of foreground and background samples. The Magic Extractor is pretty smart so you don't have to identify all of the colors in either the foreground or background. In fact, if you put in a ton of samples with the Foreground and Background Brush tool it slows down the time it takes to generate a preview considerably—especially if it is a large image (such as 3000 by 2000 pixels).

Use dots or short strokes rather than filling in a large area. Again, long brushstrokes or filling in a area with brushstrokes makes for a large number of samples for the Magic Extractor to analyze, increasing the preview time.

Zoom in on problem areas. This is especially true when working on hair. When you get a closer view you can more accurately identify foreground and background areas. Don't forget when zooming in to change to a smaller brush size. The default 20 pixel brush is pretty huge when you zoom in close.

Use your Zoom and Hand tools like a pro. To zoom in on an area, click the Zoom tool and drag a rectangle around the area to be worked on. To move to another location while zoomed in, hold down the space bar and the cursor becomes a Hand. While holding down the space bar you can pan the image within the dialog box window to get to another area on the image without changing the zoom setting. Double-clicking the Hand tool at any time changes the zoom view settings to show the entire image in the preview window.

Swap between Display choices to evaluate the image. The Display setting in the Preview setting allows you to see the Selection Area (all of the background removed) or the Original Photo. Oftentimes when a photo looks like all of the background has been successfully removed, a preview set to Original Photo reveals that someone's hair, ear, or arm has been removed as well.

Swap between different backgrounds to evaluate how clean the selection is. Adobe put a lot of different color and types of preview backgrounds in the Preview so find a background color that shows how clean the selection is and if it needs any additional work.

Be cautious with Touch-up values. The edges of selections can look ragged so there are two tools that reduce the ragged appearance—but beware. Feathering softens the edges, which sounds good but if applied at too high of a setting it results in fuzzy edges on the foreground subjects. Defringing attempts to remove any remaining background along the edge of the selection. This tool is quite aggressive so it will often remove the effects of the feathering.

Replacing the Background with Magic Extractor

Here is a good exercise to give you some practice with removing and replacing the background in a family portrait. You will need the file **Family.psd** from the Peachpit Press Web site to do this first exercise. The background in this photo is distracting. It is a living room wall with part of painting showing, as well as some cast shadows produced by the flash.

1. Open the file **family.psd** and launch the Magic Extractor (Image, Magic Extractor).

2. Use the Foreground Brush tool to select samples of colors that are present in the subject and then select the Background Brush tool to pick samples of colors and/or textures in the background. **Figure 6.16 top** shows some of the choices I made (it took less than a minute). Click the Preview button and after a few moments most of the background disappears (**Figure 6.16 bottom**).

3. At this point you need to fine-tune the selection. In my example, the area between mom and dad's heads needs some work (**Figure 6.17 top**) so I use the Zoom tool (reducing the brush size to 8 pixels so it will fit between their heads) and apply additional background samples. The results appear when clicking the Preview button (**Figure 6.17 bottom**).

4. Once all remaining areas are cleaned up, apply a low Defringe setting (1 or 2) and then apply a Feather setting of 1 pixel (px) (**Figure 6.18**, page 153).

5. When you are satisfied with the results, click OK and the original image appears without the background (**Figure 6.19**, page 153).

You could use almost any photo to serve as the replacement background for the image. In my example I used one of my fall color photos for a background (**Figure 6.20**, page 154).

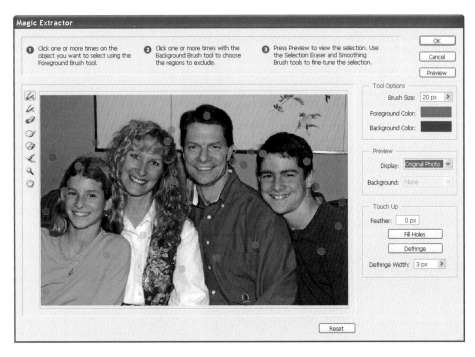

Figure 6.16
The photo shown with the original background (top). The Preview shows the background removed (bottom).

Figure 6.17
The area between the heads needs additional correction (top). The Preview shows the background is now removed, but the edges appear jagged (bottom).

Figure 6.18
Applying Feathering (1 pixel) smoothes the edges.

Figure 6.19
The photo has the background removed by the Magic Extractor.

Figure 6.20
With the background removed, another photo can be put in its place.

A Major Photo Overhaul

Before I begin showing you some fun effects let's use some of Elements' tools to turn a so-so photograph into a great one. You will need the file **Flower_boy.psd** (**Figure 6.21**) and **Clouds.jpg** to do this exercise. Here are the items that need to be corrected:

- Bluish color cast caused by an overcast sky.

- Time/date stamp needs to be removed.

- Replace the background so you can see the flower he is not giving the photographer (mommy)

1. Open the file **Flower_boy.psd**. The image is mildly over-exposed so open the Levels dialog (Ctrl+L). Change the center (midtone) setting from 0 to 0.8 (**Figure 6.22**).

2. Apply color correction to remove the blue color cast by selecting Enhance, Adjust Color, Adjust Color for Skin Tone. Click the eyedropper cursor on the darker part of the boy's cheek and click OK (**Figure 6.23**).

Figure 6.21
A cute photo but it needs some work.

Figure 6.22
Adjust the Levels to correct a minor overexposure.

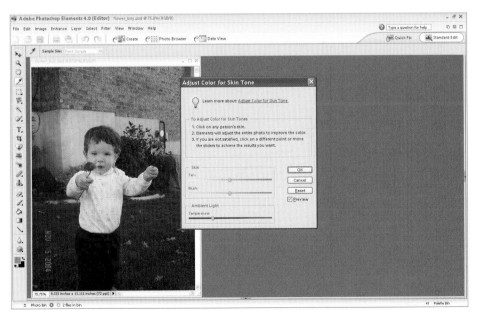

Figure 6.23
The Adjust Color for Skin Tone corrects the blue color cast.

3. To remove the time/date stamp, select the Rectangular Marquee tool in the Toolbox. In the Options bar change the Feather to 4 pixels. Drag a rectanglular shape that is roughly the same shape and size as the time/date stamp in the area as shown in **Figure 6.24**.

Figure 6.24
Create a rectangle to capture the grass that will cover the time/date stamp.

4. Select the Move tool (V). Hold down the Alt key and move the grass rectangle over the time/date stamp (**Figure 6.25**). Deselect the selection by pressing Ctrl+D.

Figure 6.25
The time/date stamp is replaced with grass.

5. Select the Magnetic Lasso tool in the Toolbox and create a selection around the boy and his flowers (**Figure 6.26**). It's not too difficult—it took me about five minutes. If you don't want to invest the time, however, I included the selection I created inside the image. To load it, choose Select, Load Selection and select Coop outline (Why Coop? His name is Cooper).

6. Convert the boy in the selection into a layer by pressing Ctrl+J. Nothing will appear to have changed at this point. Select the Polygonal Lasso tool and make the selection as shown in **Figure 6.27** (across the top of the photograph). Next select the background and add a new layer by clicking the New Layer icon. Choose the Selection Brush tool in the Toolbox and change the bottom edge as shown (**Figure 6.28**).

Figure 6.26
Select the young boy with
the Magnetic Lasso tool.

Figure 6.27
Create a Polygonal Lasso selection to contain the replacement background.

Figure 6.28
Use the Selection Brush tool to soften the lower edge of the selection.

7. Open **clouds.jpg**, and select the photo (Ctrl+A). Copy the image into the clipboard (Ctrl+C). Close **clouds.jpg** without saving the changes.

8. In the Layers palette select the new empty layer. Paste the clipboard into the selection (Ctrl+V). The cloud appears as shown in **Figure 6.29**. Use the Move tool to reposition the clouds as shown in **Figure 6.30**.

9. The grass at the horizon doesn't look real— it looks like someone stuck a grass mat up against a sky backdrop or the child is standing dangerously close to a cliff. To solve this optical dilemma, select the Blur tool from the Toolbox, and then change the strength to 100%. Select the background and blur the grass near the clouds.

10. To finish up, flatten the image by choosing Layer, Flatten Image. Deselect the image (Ctrl+D). Open Hue/Saturation (Ctrl+U), increase the Saturation to +20, and click OK (**Figure 6.31**).

Now let's see what cool stuff can be done using just the Adjustment layers.

Figure 6.29
Paste the cloud photo into the selection.

Figure 6.30
Adjust the position of the replacement sky.

Figure 6.31
The finished photo.

Isolating Colors for Effect

A favorite effect these days is to either remove all color from a photo and then selectively restore some of the colors to their original vivid hues, or replace the colors with slightly desaturated ones to make the photo appear hand-painted. It may sound complicated, but in truth both techniques are quite simple.

Removing and Restoring Color

You will need the file **Little_girl_with_pink_bow.jpg** to do this first exercise. Here is how to remove and restore color from a photo:

1. Open the file **Little_girl_with_pink_bow.jpg** (**Figure 6.32**).

2. Choose Layer, New Adjustment Layer, Hue/Saturation. Use the default name and click OK. This opens the Hue Saturation dialog. Slide the Saturation slider all the

way to the left and click OK. All color appears to be removed from the photo (**Figure 6.33**). Actually, the colors are still on the photo, but the Adjustment layer prevents them from being seen.

Figure 6.32
The original photo.

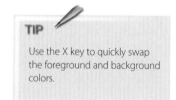

Figure 6.33
Add a Hue/Saturation Adjustment layer.

3. Select the Hue/Saturation Adjustment layer thumbnail in the Adjustment layer. Press the X key to make the foreground color black if needed. Select the Brush tool in the Toolbox and paint the areas on the photo where you wish to restore the colors. If you accidentally paint outside of the area you want, change the color to white and paint over it to change it back. In this exercise, I restored the color to the pink bow and her blue eyes (**Figure 6.34**).

TIP

Use the X key to quickly swap the foreground and background colors.

4. When you have finished, flatten the image (Layer, Flatten Image). The completed effect is shown in **Figure 6.35**.

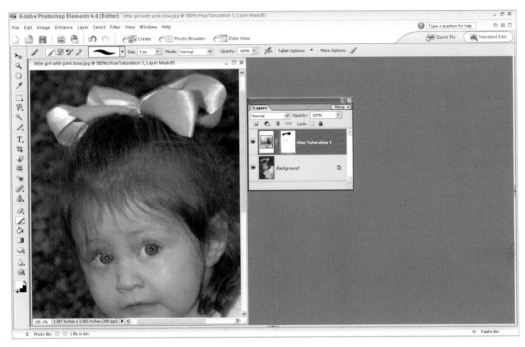

Figure 6.34
Paint the Adjustment Layer to restore the color.

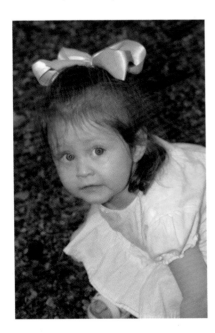

Figure 6.35
The finished photo.

Puzzling Effects

Here is a fun thing you can do with photos; make them into puzzles. The basic technique is very simple and uses a texture preset that most people don't even know is there. To do the following exercise you will need the file **Surprised_clown.jpg**.

1. Open the image **Surprised_clown.jpg** (**Figure 6.36**).

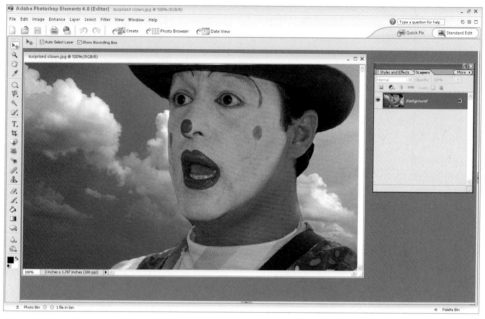

Figure 6.36
The original photo will make a good puzzle

2. Open the Texturizer filter by choosing Filter, Texture, Texturizer. Click the arrow button to the right of the Texture drop-down list and choose Load Texture from the additional options. Locate the Puzzle in the following location: Program Files/Adobe/Photoshop Elements 4.0/Presets/Textures. Apply the Puzzle texture at a setting of 150%, Relief: 10; and Light: Top Left (**Figure 6.37**).

After applying the Texture the result is shown in **Figure 6.38**.

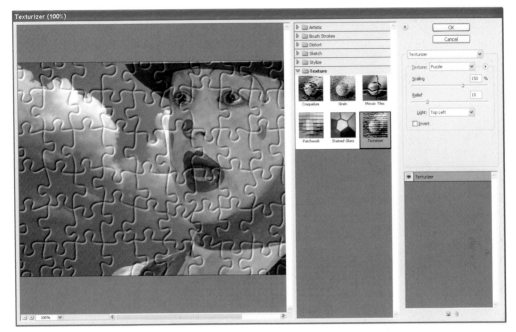

Figure 6.37
The Texturizer dialog.

Figure 6.38
The image after the puzzle texture is applied.

Fancier Puzzle Work

If you want to do more than just make a photo into a puzzle image, here is a project (**Figure 6.39**) that you can do fairly easy. I didn't make this as an exercise but I have provided enough information that you can do it.

Figure 6.39
A more advanced puzzle project.

1. Make a copy of your puzzle image and then use the Canvas Size command (Image, Resize, Canvas Resize) to increase the relative size of the image by 0.5 inch, centered on the image. A white border appears on the background (**Figure 6.40**).

2. In the Layers palette select the Background. In the Styles and Effects palette double-click the Wood Rosewood Texture Effect to apply the effect (this also create its own layer) (**Figure 6.41**).

3. To separate individual puzzle pieces, use the Magnetic Lasso tool to define a selection that follows the edge of the pieces. Once the selection is defined, make the selected piece into its own layer (Ctrl+J) as shown in **Figure 6.42**, page 168.

Figure 6.40
Add a new canvas border and a background copy.

Figure 6.41
The Rosewood effect creates a nice table for the puzzle to rest on.

Figure 6.42
Select a puzzle piece with the Magnetic Lasso tool.

4. Here is the trick of this procedure. When the selected area was made into a layer, the selection was lost. To recover the puzzle piece selection, Ctrl+click the thumbnail of the new layer and Elements creates a selection based on the transparent pixels in the layer. Make the top layer invisible. Select the layer containing the puzzle and click the Delete key to erase the selected puzzle pieces as shown in **Figure 6.43**.

5. Repeat steps 3 and 4 to make other pieces. Use Free Transformation (Ctrl+T) to rotate the individual pieces and even the original puzzle pieces. Applying Drop Shadow layer styles completes the illusion (**Figure 6.44**).

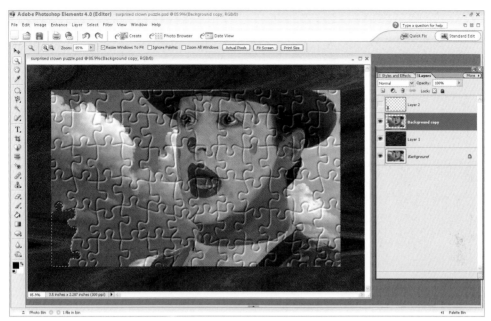

Figure 6.43
The pieces removed now make the puzzle more realistic.

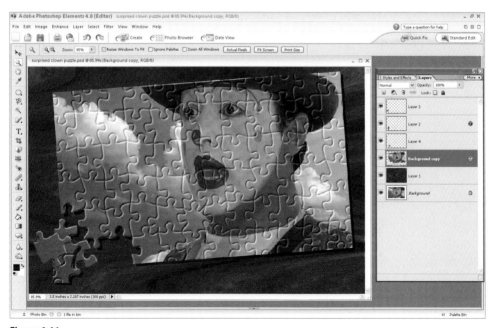

Figure 6.44
Rotating the puzzle slightly and creating multiple floating pieces is the final touch.

Creating Stunning Sunsets

The human eye is marvelous. It has the ability to capture at least ten times more shades of light and dark (called tonal dynamic range) than the most expensive digital or film camera. This is why when you take a photograph of a beautiful sunset, the foreground in the photo appears black even though you clearly see the bushes and trees in the foreground at the time you took the photograph (**Figure 6.45**).

Figure 6.45
A traditional sunset photo has a dark foreground.

Capturing with the Camera

There is a simple way to expand the ability of your camera to capture all of the dynamics of a sunset. It involves quickly taking two photos one after the other. For the best results you should use a tripod but if you are careful you can take the photos with a hand-held camera. Here's how to do it.

1. When facing the sunset, point the camera down toward the dark foreground and press the shutter button halfway. This action causes the camera to make a light reading on the darkest part of the photo. Holding down the shutter halfway causes most cameras to hold the exposure setting.

2. Still holding the shutter button down, raise the camera up and compose the image the way you want the final image to appear. Press the shutter button down the rest of the way and release it. The foreground will be properly exposed but the sunset will be greatly overexposed (**Figure 6.46**).

Figure 6.46
This photo was taken with the exposure set for the dark foreground.

3. Almost immediately press the shutter a second time. This time the camera will set its exposure based on the light of the sunset and the foreground will be very dark (**Figure 6.47**).

Figure 6.47
The bright sunset makes the foreground dark.

Combining the Photos

Once you have the photos (take lots of them), the next step is to seamlessly combine them. This will use the layer mask technique we learned earlier in the chapter. To do the exercise you need to download the images **Foreground.jpg** and **Background.jpg**. In the following technique we use the foreground as the bottom layer but you can use either photo on the bottom of the Layers palette. Here is how it is done:

1. Open the image **Foreground.jpg**. Even though the image exposure settings were correctly set for the foreground, parts of the image remain in the dark (**Figure 6.48**).

2. To bring out some detail in the foreground open Shadows/Highlights and use the default settings (**Figure 6.49**).

3. Select the Magic Wand tool, change the Tolerance setting in the Options bar to 80, and make certain that Contiguous is checked. Click on the bright overexposed sky. With the high tolerance setting the selection should fill the entire sky.

Figure 6.48
The foreground photo for the exercise.

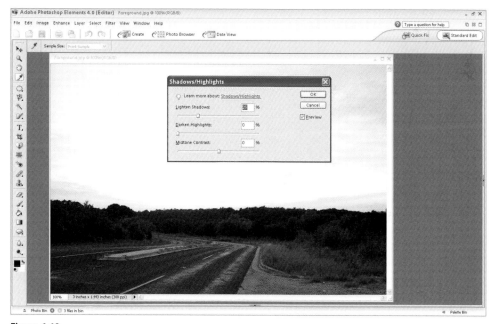

Figure 6.49
Use the Highlights/Shadow to bring out some of the detail in the foreground.

4. Now we need to create a Layer Mask. Add a new Adjustment Layer by choosing Layer, New Adjustment Layer, Levels. Name the layer Layer Mask (optional) and click OK (**Figure 6.50**).

Figure 6.50
Add a Layer mask using an Adjustment layer.

5. Open the image background. Select the entire image (Ctrl+A) and copy it to the clipboard (Ctrl+C). Close the background image.

6. Select the foreground image. Paste the background photo (Ctrl+V) on the image. The background image covers the entire image at this point. Now group the image with the Adjustment layer (Ctrl+G). The foreground is now visible (**Figure 6.51**).

7. To remove the bright edge between the foreground and the background, select the Layer mask thumbnail on the Layer mask (adjustment layer) in the Layers palette. Choose the Brush tool in the Toolbox and change the foreground color to white and paint the edge. Everywhere that you paint with white makes the darker areas of the background visible. If it becomes too dark switch the color to black and paint over the same area. When you're finished the edge will be gone and the horizon will be slightly darker as it should be (**Figure 6.52**).

8. The road at the bottom of the foreground is a little tacky. To deemphasize it, use the Brush tool at low opacity to slightly darken the road near the edges of the image (**Figure 6.53**).

Figure 6.51
When the top background layer is grouped the foreground becomes visible.

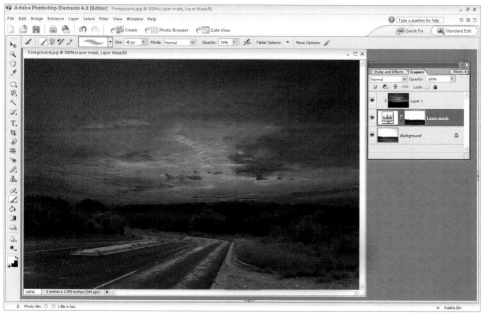

Figure 6.52
Adjusting the Layer mask removes the bright edge on the horizon.

Figure 6.53
Use the Brush tool to shade areas and to deemphasize the rather ugly road.

In the next chapter, we jump into the art form that will make your photography very popular—retouching photographs. This is the neat stuff that makes those of us who are older, look younger (which I greatly appreciate), and it also tidies up physical imperfections.

7 Fun with Type, Shapes, and Cookie Cutter Tools

Once your photos are picture-perfect—or nearly so—you can become creative with them. This chapter shows some of the amazing things that you can add to, or do, with the Type, Shape, and Cookie Cutter tools in Photoshop Elements. The Type tool lets you add text to photos for everything from titles, photo credits, and captions. The Shape tools give you the ability to create and add both geometric and custom shapes. The Cookie Cutter tool lets you quickly change a photo into a shape that you can further modify using Layer styles.

Adding Text Using the Type Tool

We'll begin by tackling the Type tool, which lets us add text to any image we are working on. Let's start with something simple, like adding some simple text, and work up to more complicated effects.

Before we begin, you need to understand an important concept about working with both text and shapes. Text and shapes are unique in Photoshop Elements because they are vector based, meaning that they are composed of mathematical paths rather than pixels. This is important for two reasons: First, the text and shapes can be resized, twisted, and distorted without any loss of quality. Second, some effects in Elements cannot be applied to a type or shape layer without first converting the layer into pixels—a process called *simplifying a layer.*

Adding text to a photo has many uses. You can add titles, descriptions, silly stuff, or copyright information. The easiest way to learn how to add text to your photos is by doing it. To work with text you must have a working knowledge of the Layers palette.

The Layers Palette

The Layers palette allows you to see text and images that are on separate layers. Think of layers as analogous to the sheets of clear acetate that are used with overhead projectors. If you have drawn an object on one layer (or sheet), you can move it around independently of the objects drawn on the other layers (or sheets). The parts of the Layers palette we will be using in this chapter are identified in **Figure 7.1** for your reference.

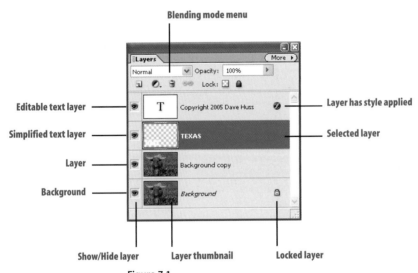

Figure 7.1
The Layers palette lets you see and control the layers in an image.

To open the Layers palette, go to the Window menu and choose Layers to view the Layers palette. If the palette is not docked in the Palette Bin, drag the Layers tab into the Palette Bin to save space on your screen. You can group the Layers (or any) palette into the Palette Bin by dragging its tag into the Palette Bin.

TIP

I recommend the Layers palette always be visible while working with text and shapes.

How to Add Single-Line Text

The first example (**Figure 7.2**) uses a photo of a longhorn steer in a field of bluebonnets, which can be downloaded from the Peachpit Press Web site. In this first exercise you will only add a single line of text. When you type new text, it appears on a new type layer. You can create single-line text or paragraph text. (We'll learn more about paragraph text in the next section.) Each line of single-line text you enter is independent—the length of a line grows or shrinks as you edit it, but it doesn't wrap to the next line (like paragraph text does).

1. Open **Longhorn.jpg**.

2. Select the Horizontal Type tool (T) in the Toolbox, in the Tool Options bar (**Figure 7.3**) change the font to Impact, and the size to 72 pt (points). Place the cursor on the image and it changes into a text bar.

Figure 7.2
Longhorn steer in a field of bluebonnets.

Type tool

Horizontal Type tool

Font   **Size**   **Font color**

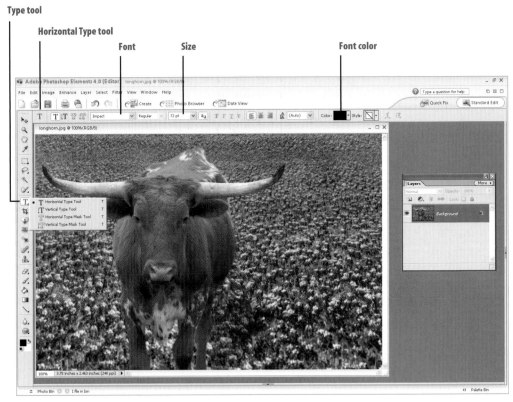

Figure 7.3
Select the Horizontal Type tool.

3. When you have finished entering or editing text, click the Commit check mark icon at the end of the Options bar (**Figure 7.4**).

4. After inserting the text, a Type layer appears in the Layers palette floating above the Background layer, as shown in **Figure 7.5**. As long as the text remains a Type layer, you can go back and edit it.

5. Use the Font Color Picker in the Tools Options bar to choose a color for the text. You can also change text color by selecting the Type tool, then selecting the Type layer in the Layers palette, and then clicking on the Foreground color and choosing your new color from the Color Picker. You can also put the cursor over the photo and pick a color from the photo. In this case, I picked a burnt orange from the back of the longhorn steer (**Figure 7.6**, page 182).

Cancel Commit

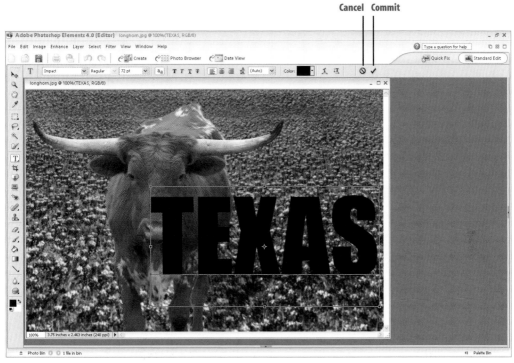

Figure 7.4
The Cancel and Commit icons.

The result is shown in **Figure 7.7**. That's all that is necessary to place text in a photo. If you think you will want to make any changes to the text at a later date, then use File, Save As and choose Photoshop or TIFF as the format. This way the text remains as an editable Type layer. If you don't think you will ever want to make changes, or if you want to send this as an e-mail message, you need to flatten the layer (Layer, Flatten Image) and save it as a JPEG.

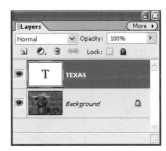

Figure 7.5
The text is now floating as an editable Type layer.

Figure 7.6
Define the color using the Color Picker.

Figure 7.7
Bluebonnets and a longhorn; the text is almost redundant.

Creating Paragraph Text

Paragraph text is a new feature in Photoshop Elements 4 that automatically wraps the text around the text box. Before this feature was added to Elements, the only way to create paragraph text was to compose the paragraph of multiple single lines of text, which is complicated and difficult to manage.

The next exercise uses the photo **Flag.jpg**, which can be downloaded from the Peachpit Press Web site.

1. Open **Flag.jpg** and use the Rectangular Marquee tool (M) to create a selection similar to the one shown in **Figure 7.8**.

> **TIP**
>
> You can change the angle and depth of the shadow by double-clicking on the Layer style icon in the Layers palette and changing the settings.

2. Open the Styles and Effect palette by choosing Window, Styles and Effects. Double-click the thumbnail of the Text Panel (selection) effect in the Effects part of the palette. This creates a transparent shape with a drop shadow (**Figure 7.9**, next page).

3. Select the Type tool in the Toolbox and drag a rectangle that is the size of the text box. Change the alignment to Centered in the Tool Options bar and enter any text you choose (**Figure 7.10**, next page). When complete, click the Commit icon.

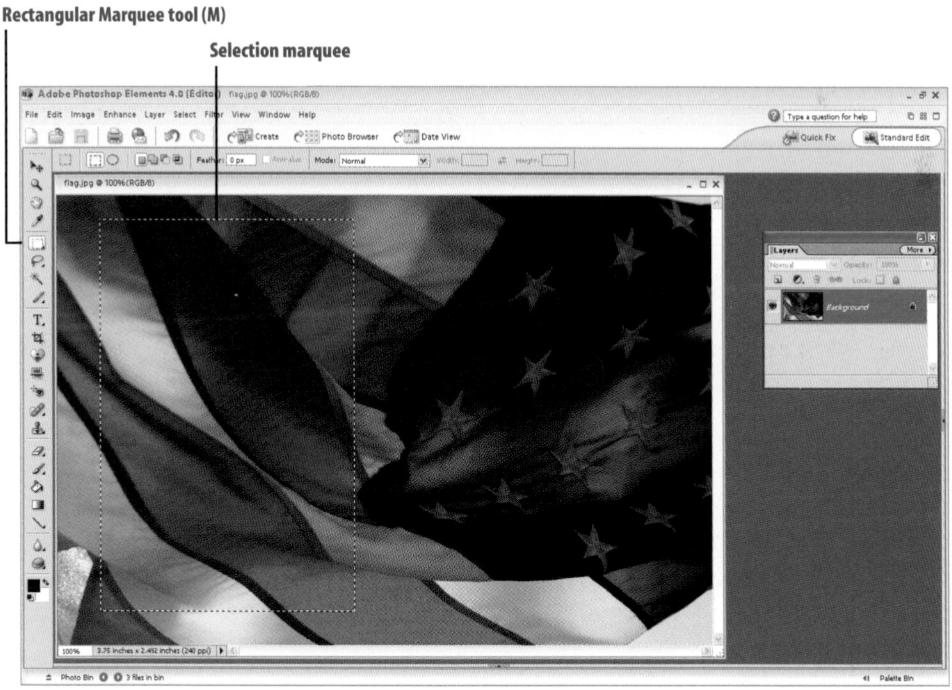

Rectangular Marquee tool (M)

Selection marquee

Figure 7.8
Define a Rectangular selection.

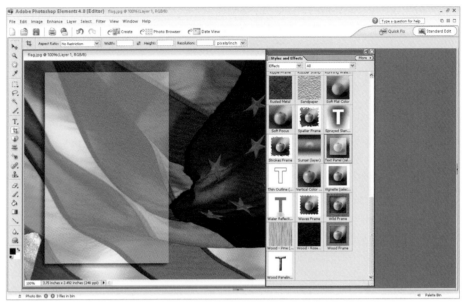

Figure 7.9
Apply the Text Panel Layer Effect to serve as a backdrop for the text.

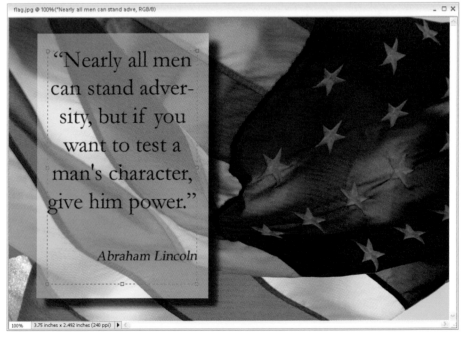

Figure 7.10
Add a great quotation.

4. Often the text will not break where you want it. You can change where the text breaks by inserting hard returns. In this example I didn't like that the word "adversity" was on two lines. To correct it, place the cursor in front of the word and then press the Enter key. Now the word "character" is split on two lines and "Abraham Lincoln" has disappeared (**Figure 7.11**).

5. Putting a hard return in front of "character" removed the break but Lincoln is still pushed out of the text box. Instead of making the text smaller, reduce the leading (space between the lines) in the Tools Options bar. With the Type tool selected insert it someplace in the text. Select all of the text (Ctrl+A). Change the leading from Auto to 14 pt (points). The reduced leading allows all of the text to appear (**Figure 7.12**).

6. Finish up by removing the extra space between the quote and Lincoln. Select the Move tool (V) and resize the box vertically to fit the text and position it in the box, as shown in **Figure 7.13**, next page.

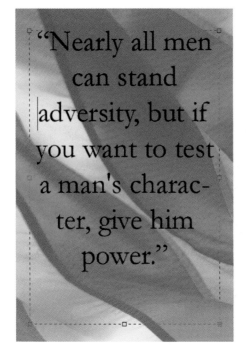

Figure 7.11
Use the new paragraph text feature to resize and reposition the text.

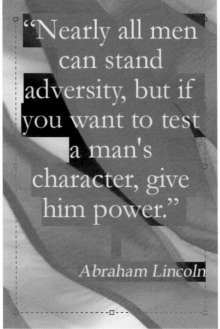

Figure 7.12
The paragraph text still needs adjustment.

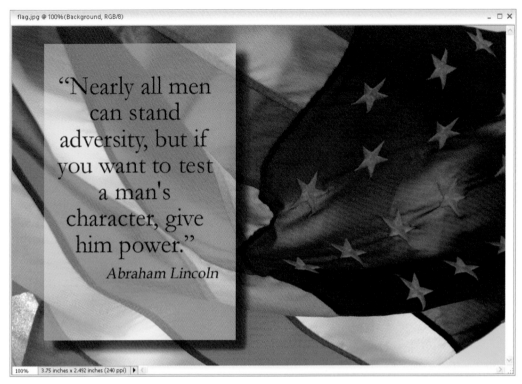

Figure 7.13
The completed work.

Editing and Formatting Text

Editing text on a Text layer is relatively straightforward. If you want to change the text, simply choose the Type tool, click in the text area where you want to make changes, and then add or delete the necessary text. The Escape key cancels out any changes you make to your text. (In other words, if you change your mind and decide you don't like the changes, the Escape key is your best friend.) The Commit icon in the Tool Options bar applies any changes that are made to text.

The basic text formatting options include the following:

- **Font Options.** Font, style, and size are all controlled in the Options bar. Their operation is pretty self-explanatory. By default, type size is displayed in points (72 pts = 1 inch).

- **Leading.** Leading provides the ability to control the spacing between lines. Found in the Options bar, this only works when the text you enter covers several lines and the text is selected (highlighted).

- **Color.** The color of the selected type is determined by the current foreground color. When you are adding text, there are two ways to control the color:

  - Clicking the down arrow next to the Color option in the Type Options bar opens the Color menu, a palette of pre-set colors (**Figure 7.14**).

  - If you want to use the Color Picker (**Figure 7.15**), you can open it by clicking the Color swatch in the Options bar, and clicking the More Colors button in the Color menu, or clicking the Foreground Color swatch in the Toolbox. To select a color with the Color Picker, drag the vertical color slider until the color field displays the range of colors you are seeking. Next, click in the color field. A circular marker indicates the color's position in the field, and the adjusted color swatch reflects the new color. Click the OK button to accept the color. To learn about the other options on the Color Picker, click the Choosing Colors help link.

Opens Color Picker   Click to open Color menu

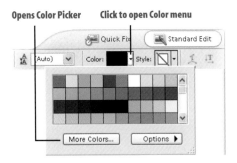

Figure 7.14
The abbreviated Color Picker in the Text Options bar.

TIP

Moving the cursor outside of the Color menu or the Color Picker dialog turns it into an eyedropper, allowing you to select a font color using one that exists in the photo you are working on or any other photo that is open.

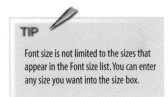

TIP

Font size is not limited to the sizes that appear in the Font size list. You can enter any size you want into the size box.

Color field   Color Picker Help   Adjusted color   Original color

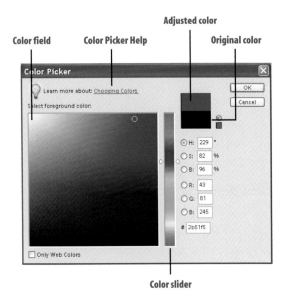

Color slider

Figure 7.15
The standard Color Picker dialog.

Quick and Easy Ways to Change Text

To avoid the hassle of first highlighting the text, just click the Type layer in the Layers palette and, with the Type tool active, make the changes on the Options bar (**Figure 7.16**). Your changes are applied universally to all the text in that layer only.

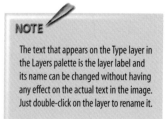

NOTE

The text that appears on the Type layer in the Layers palette is the layer label and its name can be changed without having any effect on the actual text in the image. Just double-click on the layer to rename it.

Select Type tool   Make type changes on Options bar   Select Type layer

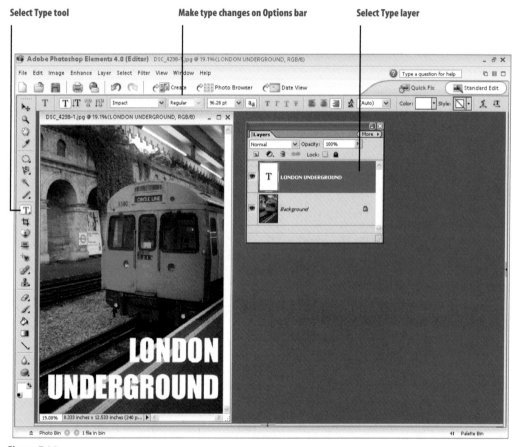

Figure 7.16
The Type tool options.

Making Twisted Type with Warp Text

In addition to controlling the size of type and the spacing between the lines, you can also change the overall shape of the type by using Warp Text. This feature allows you to apply any one of the 15 different presets in the Warp Text Style menu. Warp Text only works on text and there are many effects you can apply using it. Here is a basic example of how it works:

1. While the Type tool is still active, highlight the text and click the Create Warped Text icon in the Options bar, which opens the Warp Text dialog box (**Figure 7.17**).

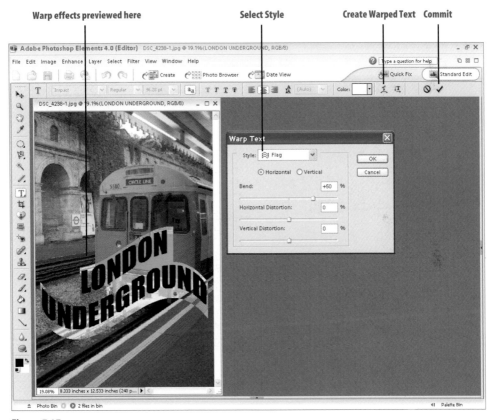

Figure 7.17
The Warp Text tool.

2. After selecting a Style, use the controls to manipulate the degree and direction of warping. The effects are previewed in the image.

3. When the text appears the way you want it to, click OK, then click the Commit check mark in the Options bar.

4. Before you can apply any effects, paint, or layer styles you must first render the text. Add color, as well as a Bevel Layer and a Drop Shadow style, as shown in **Figure 7.18**, and you have a favorite slogan here in Texas.

Figure 7.18
The Warp Text tool provides an endless variety of text effects.

Wrap Text Using Warped Type

Here is an exercise to show one of the many uses for warped text. In a world that has debased my drug of choice, coffee, into a Styrofoam-wrapped concoction, I thought it would be fun to use a photo of a real coffee cup.

1. Download and open the file **Coffee_cup.jpg**.

2. Select the Type tool and change the font to Impact at 30 points, the font color to white, the alignment to centered, and the leading to 30 points.

3. Enter the text, "COFFEE is my drug of choice," as shown in **Figure 7.19**.

4. Click the Create Warped Text icon and when the Warp Text dialog opens, change the Style to Arc. Change the following settings in the Warp Text dialog: Bend to -27%, Horizontal Distortion to 0%, and Vertical Distortion to -33%. Click the OK button and the Commit check mark in the Options bar. The resulting text should look like that shown in **Figure 7.20**.

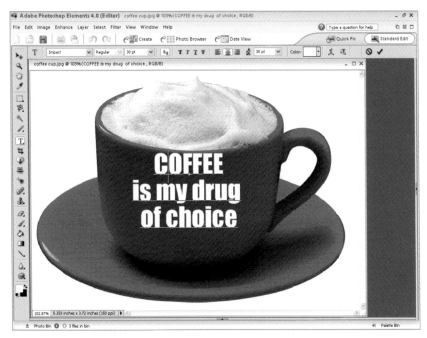

Figure 7.19
Add text to be wrapped around the cup.

Figure 7.20
Use Warp Text to fit the text around the cup.

5. The white type is too bright. To make it look more realistic, we need to shade it. To prepare, go to the Layers palette, right-click the Type layer and choose Simplify Layer from the pop-up menu. Now we can apply effects to the layer containing the type. Check the Lock transparent pixels button at the top of the Layers palette as shown in **Figure 7.21**. This restricts any effects we apply to the type (opaque pixels).

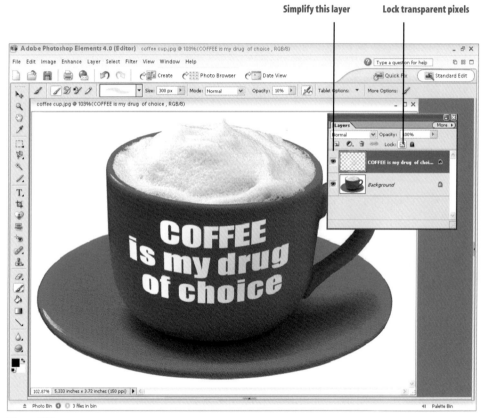

Figure 7.21
Prepare the text for shading.

6. Select the Brush tool and make the foreground color black. Make the brush size very large -300 pixels (px), change the Opacity to a very faint 10% and enable the airbrush effects. Paint the lower right part of the text to match the existing shadows on the original photograph as shown in **Figure 7.22**. The change is subtle so don't overdo it.

The completed text effect is shown in **Figure 7.23**.

Brush tool   Paint this area   Brush size   Brush opacity   Enable airbrush capabilities

Figure 7.22
Use the Brush tool to create the shading effect.

Figure 7.23
The finished cup complete with slogan.

Cool Effects Using Layer Styles

Layer styles can be used to create many effects, like very realistic drop shadows behind text, and realistic plastic, chrome, and neon type, just to name a few. Let's learn more about layer styles and see what else we can do with these wonders.

Layer styles are located in the Styles and Effects palette. The Styles and Effect palette can be opened from the Window menu, or when working with type, it be selected from the Options bar (**Figure 7.24**).

Here is one way you can apply a Style:

1. Enter some text on an image using the Type tool and finish by clicking the Commit check mark icon. The example in **Figure 7.25** is in red type.

2. Open the Styles and Effects palette. Make sure the category selector at the top left of the palette is set to Layer Styles and the Library Selector box next to it is set to Wow Plastic (**Figure 7.26**).

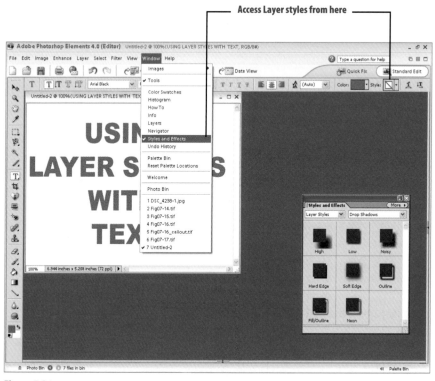

Figure 7.24
Two ways to access Layer Styles.

Figure 7.25
Apply some red text.

Figure 7.26
One of many Layer Styles found in Photoshop Elements.

3. Scroll down the palette and pick any Wow Plastic style that is not red and click it. The text changes immediately (**Figure 7.27**). A lot of the layer styles (such as the one you just used) override the selected color of the text.

Figure 7.27
Applying some layer styles changes the color of the original text or object.

Things to Know About Layer Styles

Styles can be used to create a wide variety of effects for both text and shapes (we discuss shapes next). The Photoshop Elements User Guide and the online help provide a lot of detailed information about all their ins and outs. Here are some basic things to know about using them:

- **Undoing a Style**. To undo the last application of a style, click the Step Backward icon in the shortcut bar.

- **Styles are Cumulative**. You can apply multiple styles to text or to a shape. When some styles are applied, they replace or modify the effect of similar styles. For example, in the last exercise, if any other Wow Plastic styles are applied, the new style completely replaces the existing style. If a drop shadow is applied (**Figure 7.28**), the text remains unchanged, but the new drop shadow replaces the tinted one.

- **Styles are Adjustable**. Each style can be individually adjusted after it is applied. This is most important when applying drop shadows. The next section shows how to modify the style.

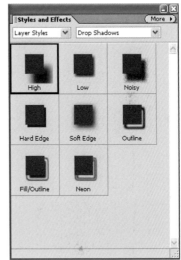

Figure 7.28
Applying a drop shadow changes the color of the shadow but not the text.

How to Modify a Style

After a style is applied to a layer, an icon appears on the right side of the layer. For example to change the drop shadow sample shown in **Figure 7.29** you must double-click the icon to open the Style Settings dialog. With Drop Shadow styles you can control the direction the light is coming from (Lighting Angle) and how far the shadow appears from the text or shape (Shadow Distance). The other controls may be grayed out because they are used by the drop shadow.

Styles are real time-wasters. By that, I mean there is so much you can do with them, you will end up spending a lot of time just playing with them. I have created a small sampling of a few of the styles in **Figure 7.30**. The images at the bottom are made using shapes, which is the next topic.

Layer Style icon

Figure 7.29
A layer style can be modified after clicking the icon in the Layers palette.

Figure 7.30
Several examples of what can be achieved using the Layer Styles feature.

Using Shapes in Your Photos

A feature in Photoshop Elements that is similar to the Type tool are the Shape tools, which are used to create all types of geometric and custom shapes. The control and configuration of these tools are covered in painful detail in both the Elements 4 User Guide and in the online help. In this section of the chapter, we will learn how to do some cool things with the tools.

Adding Comic Book Balloons to Photos

Earlier in this chapter, we covered the topic of adding text over a photo. Now, using the Custom Shape tool, we'll learn how to make the subject speak by adding a comic book-style balloon to the image. Here is how it's done:

1. Download and open the file **Baby.jpg (Figure 7.31)**.

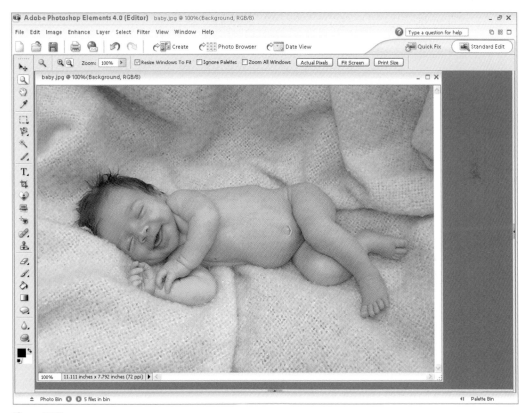

Figure 7.31
As cute as this baby is, we can make the photo even cuter with text.

2. Select the Shape tool (U) in the Toolbox. From the Options bar click the Custom Shape tool (**Figure 7.32**), and then click the down arrow next to the Shape option to open the Custom Shape picker.

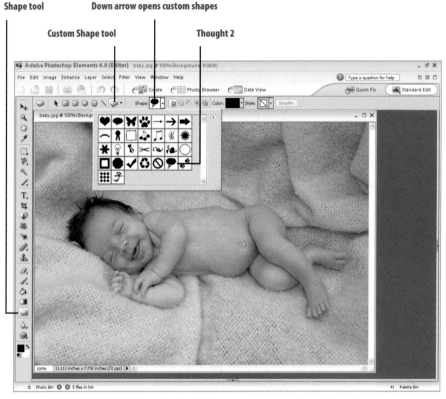

Figure 7.32
Open the Custom Shape option.

3. Select the thought balloon near the bottom of the list (Thought 2). Change the foreground color to white. Somewhere near the baby's head, click and drag a shape like the one shown in **Figure 7.33**. A Shape layer has been added to the Layers palette.

4. Select the Type tool and change the font to Comic Sans MS at a size of 24 points and Bold. The leading should be set to Auto. If the Auto setting creates line spacing that is too large to fit into the thought balloon, you can change it to any value. Enter the text and click the Commit check mark (**Figure 7.34**).

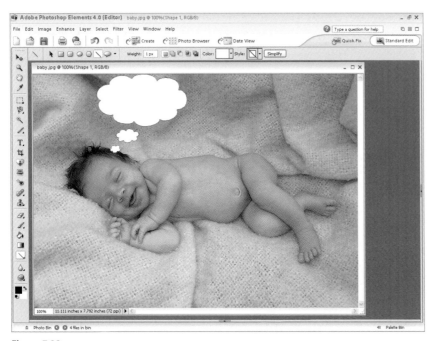

Figure 7.33
Add a thought balloon.

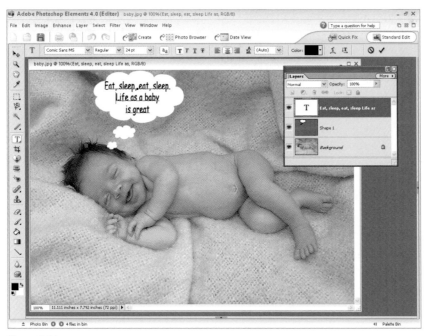

Figure 7.34
Add some thoughts to the thought balloon.

Identifying Parts of a Photo with Shapes

Shape tools are great for identifying parts of a photograph. The uses are almost limitless whether it's showing a specific location on a circuit board for a science project (**Figure 7.35**) or something silly (**Figure 7.36**).

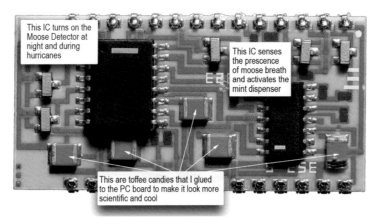

Figure 7.35
Shapes are a good way to identify areas and parts—even silly ones.

Figure 7.36
Shapes don't have to be white.

The rectangles in Figure 7.35 are made with the Rectangle Shape tool. Making lines with arrowheads is not as obvious. Here is how it's done:

1. Select the Line shape tool in the Shape tool Options bar (**Figure 7.37**).

2. Click the Geometry Options button. By checking or unchecking Start and End for Arrowheads, you can determine if lines drawn using the Line Shape tool have arrowheads or not.

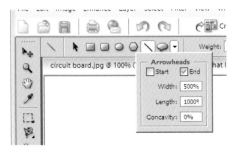

Figure 7.37
Arrowheads on lines can be edited from the Options bar.

Simplifying Type and Shape Layers

When you attempt to apply an effect that cannot be applied to a vector layer, Photoshop Elements warns you that the layer must first be converted to a bitmap layer (simplifying the layer) by displaying a warning box like the one shown in **Figure 7.38**. Clicking OK will simplify the layer and apply the effect. Two important things to remember when simplifying a type or shape layer are that it will no longer be editable after it is simplified, and that the text and shapes on a vector layer print out much sharper after the layer has been simplified.

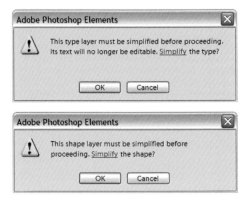

Figure 7.38
These warnings occur if you attempt to apply effects to layers before they are simplified.

Combining Type, Shapes, and Photos

When making cover or title pages that really get the viewer's attention, you need to get a little creative, and Elements has the tools to let you do just that.

The disadvantage of using any type mask is that once the selection is created, it is very difficult to make changes to the shape. To be able to resize and twist the shapes of these photo-filled characters after they are created, we need to use a little-known feature in Photoshop Elements that allows you to fill type or shapes with a photo. Technically, it's called a clipping mask, and it uses Type layers or Shape layers to control what parts of a photo the viewer sees. Rather than spend a paragraph explaining it, let's see how it works. If you want to follow along, download the file **Wildflowers.jpg**.

1. Open the photo and select the Type tool.

2. Enter the text you want to fill with the flowers. The example in **Figure 7.39** was made using the Impact font initially at a size of 60 points and leading of 60 points. After the type was in place, I used the Move tool (V) to stretch the text to fill the screen.

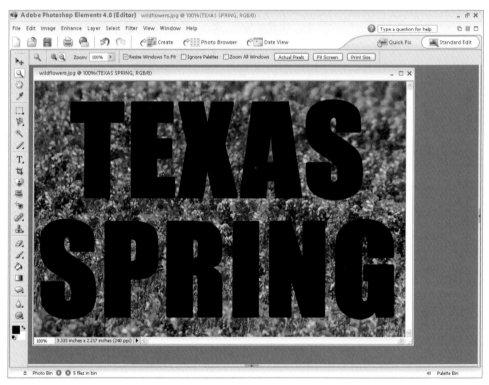

Figure 7.39
Place text on the photo.

3. Make a Background copy layer by clicking and dragging the background in the Layers palette onto the New Layer icon (**Figure 7.40**).

4. Select Background (not Background copy) in the Layers palette, choose Edit, Fill Layer, and then choose Use White to clear the original flower background.

5. Drag the Type layer so that it is between the Background and the Background copy layer. The text disappears.

6. Select the Background copy layer in the Layers palette, and in the Layers menu, select Group with Previous (Ctrl+G) and see the results (**Figure 7.42**).

7. Apply the Simple Inner Bevel and the Low Drop Shadow styles to the Type layer from the Styles and Effects palette, and the text takes on a nice, finished appearance (**Figure 7.43**, next page).

Figure 7.40
Make a copy of the background.

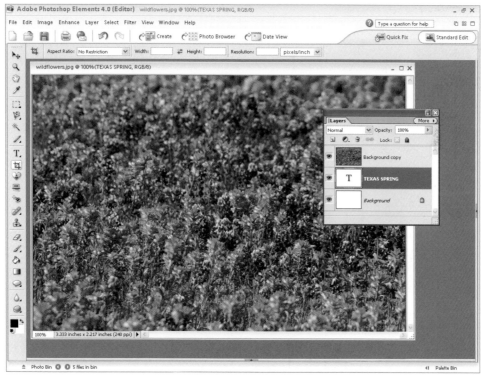

Figure 7.41
Move the background copy on top.

Figure 7.42
Group the top layer with the text.

Figure 7.43
Apply Layer Styles to complete the effect.

A Sample CD Cover

To demonstrate what can be done with Elements, I have used a few of the techniques discussed in the chapter to create a CD insert (**Figure 7.44**). The background is a close-up photo I took of a fencepost (which we have lots of in Texas). The band's name—Twisted Wire—was applied using the mask technique used in the "Texas Spring" exercise. The album name, *Range War*, was made using regular type to which both the Simple Emboss and the Soft Shadow styles were applied.

How Does Group with Previous Work?

After Group with Previous is applied, the Type layer becomes a clipping mask, which makes everything on the top layer transparent, except for the areas where the typed black letters appear. The top layer is still all there—you just can't see parts of it. You can change the size or shape of the text on the Type layer or apply some of the Style layers to it, and it will affect the appearance.

TIP

So when you are adding a lot of text to an image, wouldn't it be great to have a spell checker? Yes it would. So where is the spelling checker? It's not in this version of Elements—maybe in Elements 5. So, how do you check your spelling? Type the text you want to enter in either your favorite word processor or the program you use to send e-mails and run its spell checker. Once the spelling is correct, select and copy the text to the clipboard (Ctrl+C), and then after selecting the Type tool, paste (Ctrl+V) the text into the image.

Figure 7.44
The tools in Elements allow you to create professional images like this CD insert.

Using the Cookie Cutter Tool

The Cookie Cutter tool was a new addition to Photoshop Elements 3. It is a great tool that scrapbookers will love that is very easy to use. With it you can reshape the borders of any photograph into a custom shape. The tool uses the shapes from the custom shapes we already saw when we looked at the Shapes tools. The difference between the Cookie Cutter and the Custom Shape tools is that the Cookie Cutter tool turns the photo into the shape of the custom shape you chose. **Figure 7.45** shows the location of the Cookie Cutter tool and the Options that control how the shape responds when the shape is dragged out.

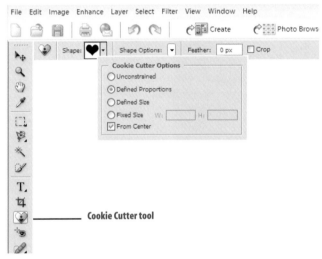

Figure 7.45
The Cookie Cutter tool and Options bar open.

Here is how the Cookie Cutter tool works:

1. Open the file, **Laughing.jpg** (**Figure 7.46**).

2. Select the Cookie Cutter tool in the Toolbox and choose one of the crop shapes from the Options bar. The one used is Crop Shape 30 (the name appears as you place the cursor over the shape). To see all of the many shapes included, you must click the More Options button in the upper-right of the box as shown in **Figure 7.47**. Once you have clicked on the shape, click and drag the shape over the photo.

Figure 7.46
Why is this girl laughing?

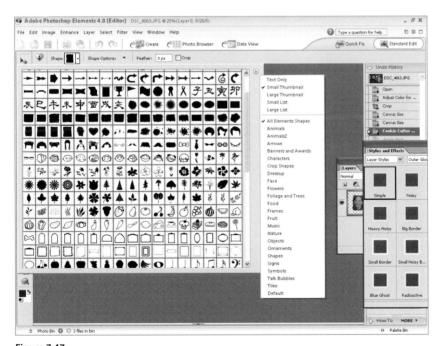

Figure 7.47
Using the More Options button reveals a large number of custom shapes.

3. As soon as the mouse button is released, the area outside of the shape is removed (**Figure 7.48**). Click the Commit check mark to complete the action.

4. Select Gold Sprinkles from the Effects category in the Styles and Effects palette. The effect creates a gold layer on top of the photo (**Figure 7.49**).

5. In the Layer palette drag the Gold Sprinkles layer below the Cookie Cutter layer. **Figure 7.50** shows the effect.

Figure 7.48
Use the Cookie Cutter crop shape to create a rough edge.

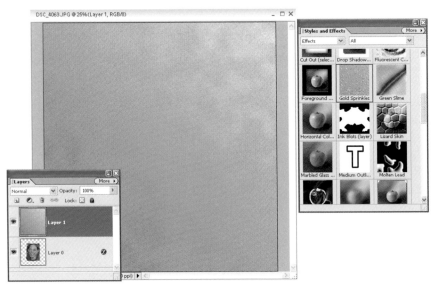

Figure 7.49
Add a Layer Style on top of the Cookie Cutter image.

Figure 7.50
Move the Cookie Cutter image on top.

6. Move the Cookie Cutter layer up to make room for a caption. Using the Color Picker, you can pick a maroon color for the type by placing the cursor on the neckline of her shirt. After adding the caption, apply a border around the edge using the Style named Outer Glow. To complete the project, just flatten the Layer (Layer, Flatten Image), and you're finished (**Figure 7.51**).

Figure 7.51
Add text with Layer Styles to complete the image.

This chapter's goal was to provide you with basic text-handling concepts, and to develop the skills that will increase your confidence when tackling personal projects. We covered many (but not all) of the cool things you can do with Type, Shapes, and even the Cookie Cutter tool. Somewhere along the way, maybe you even discovered that "Oh, wow!" factor while working with this program. In the next chapter, you'll learn some retouching tips and tricks that will make your photos look even more professional.

8 Retouching Photos Like a Pro

Cameras can be cruel devices in that they capture images with frightening clarity. Unless you are a member of the camera-toting paparazzi (who appear to enjoy making celebrities look as bad as possible), when most of us take a photograph of someone, we want to capture an expression reflective of the individual's personality. We want to capture a moment in time in a photograph. The camera has no such agenda. It faithfully captures every wrinkle, mole, scar, and blemish on the subject. It can also, with an uncanny ability, discover double chins where none before existed, bulging tummies, shiny noses and faces, yellowed teeth, and blood-shot eyes in a teetotaler.

What makes the camera so mean? It isn't mean; it can only faithfully record what it sees. We, as humans, on the other hand, tend to tune out these physical aberrations when we are with the subject. However, it is difficult to overlook them later when looking at the photograph you took.

Why do I mention this? Because this chapter is devoted to using Photoshop Elements to make your photos of people and other subjects look better, and not necessarily look the way the camera records them. If you are a photojournalist (paparazzi are not photojournalists), quit reading now because this chapter is devoted to the one subject you are opposed to—changing reality.

Preparing for Retouching

You will learn as you go through this chapter that in most situations, retouching a photo requires working at high zoom levels. For example, the first exercise in this chapter requires zooming in very close to remove the braces from a woman's teeth. It is difficult to see the changes on the entire image when working at that high of a magnification. Fortunately, Elements has provided an excellent solution called View New Window.

1. Open the image that you will be working on.

2. Choose View, New Window for (filename) (**Figure 8.1**).

3. A second window with the image opens (**Figure 8.2**). Any changes made to the original image instantly appear in the new window. Using the Zoom tool (Z) you can zoom in and out of the original, while the zoom setting of the new window remains unaffected. Even though both windows are showing the same image, you can change the zoom settings on each one independently.

Figure 8.1
Open a New Window from the View menu.

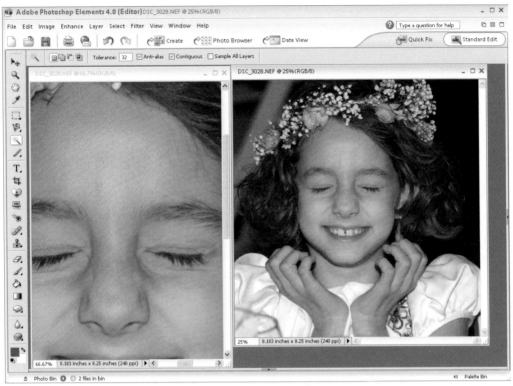

Figure 8.2
The second, new window allows you to see "the whole picture" while working on an area at high magnification.

Removing Braces

We begin with some common and not-too-difficult photo fix-ups that I run into all of the time—thus creating glamour shots. By glamour shots I mean removing blemishes, braces, whitening teeth, and eyes. I take a lot of photos of kids because they make great subjects and I've yet to encounter a five-year old who shields her face with her hands saying, "Don't take my picture! I'm not wearing makeup." When they get older, that all changes. The photo of the two young ladies in **Figure 8.3** is fine, except my daughter doesn't like her braces appearing in photos.

TIP

Using the New Window feature, you can open up multiple new windows on a single image. The only limitations on how many images can be open are the physical size of your screen and the amount of memory you have available.

Figure 8.3
Beautiful girls but one of them doesn't like her braces showing up in pictures.

Braces are something that appearance-conscious people want and since they are conscious of their appearance they don't want you to see them wearing braces. I was trying to do a family portrait earlier this year and one of the three daughters had braces on. Out of the family of five, she was the one with her lips sealed and as a result she looked like she might be suffering from lockjaw. It wasn't until I assured her that I would remove the braces from the photo and whiten her teeth to boot that she gave me a big smile.

In learning how to remove braces, we will be using Clone Stamp Brush. We cannot use the Healing Brush or the Spot Healing Brush because they pull the colors from the braces into the teeth.

To do the following exercise, you will need to download the image **Braces.jpg** from the Peachpit Press Web site. Let's see what we can do about removing these braces.

1. Open the file **Braces.jpg**. The first step is to zoom in on the braces. Select the Zoom tool (Z) from the Toolbox and drag a rectangle around the mouth. Your display should look like the one shown in **Figure 8.4**.

2. Create a new window of the photo so that you can see how the changes being made affect the appearance of the whole photo. Choose View, New Window for the photo. A new window of the ladies appears. Move it to another part of the screen, away from the area in which we are working and zoom it in so only the woman's face shows (**Figure 8.5**, next page).

> **NOTE**
>
> The zoom factor necessary to fit the mouth area in the window depends on the size and settings of your display. Mine was less than 200%, yours may be different.

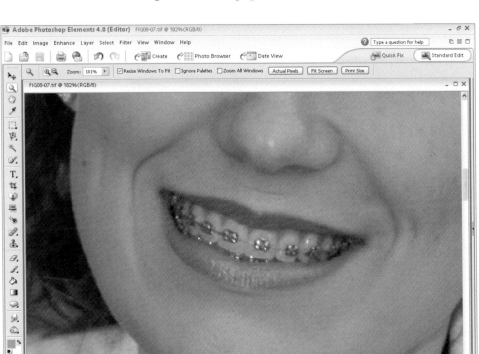

Figure 8.4
First step: zoom in on the area to be worked on.

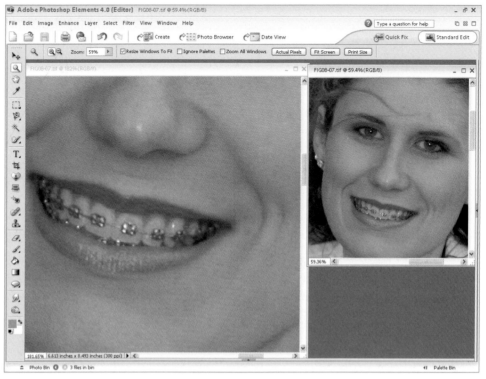

Figure 8.5
Next, make a new window to see how the changes affect the photo.

3. Select the original image. Choose the Clone Stamp Brush ![icon]. Select the Soft Round 5 pixel preset and change the settings in the Options bar to Mode: Normal, Opacity: 100%, and uncheck the Aligned box.

4. Zoom in even closer (using the thumbwheel on your mouse). First, we need to select an area of tooth we can use to cover the brace. Beginning with one of her larger front teeth, hold down the Alt key and place the cursor below the brace and click. Click the cursor on the brace. The pixels in the source area are painted onto the brace. Continue clicking on the brace until it gone (**Figure 8.6**).

> **TIP**
>
> To create more room in your crowded workspace, close the Palette Bin (Window, click on Palette Bin) if it's open.

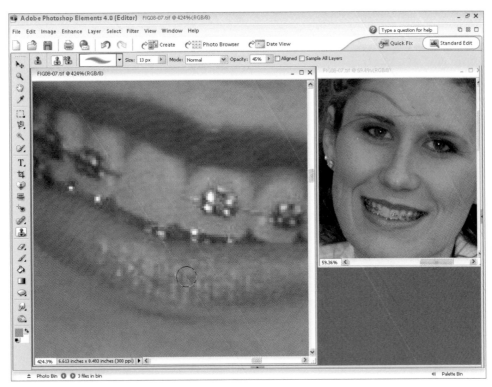

Figure 8.6
Select a source point to use for removing the braces.

5. Continue to clone the white areas of the teeth over the braces. Here are some suggestions when removing braces. Do not clone over the space between the teeth. Color in teeth is not uniform and so when removing braces I try to sample from both the tops and bottom areas of teeth. As you approach the sides of the mouth the teeth will become grayer because they are in partial shadow so find similarly colored tooth areas to use as a source. Don't make them all front-teeth white or the resulting photo will look freakily fake. Last, use the gray area between the teeth and the lower lip as a source to cover up the bright reflections off of the metal. The completed first half of the mouth should look like the one shown in **Figure 8.7**.

6. Repeat on the other side of the mouth until it looks like the one shown in **Figure 8.8** (next page). The second side takes less time because the finished side of the mouth can be used for source pixels for the Clone Stamp brush. Be patient. Removing braces takes time. As a point of reference, I assume it will take me a half an hour to remove braces from a photo.

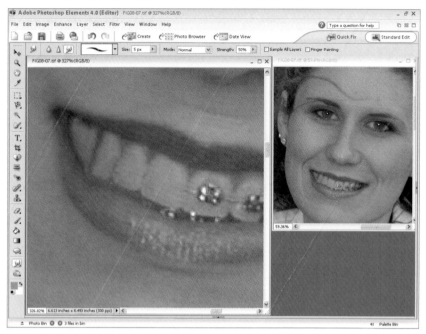

Figure 8.7
Half of the mouth has the braces removed.

Figure 8.8
All of the braces are gone.

Removing Blemishes, Whitening Teeth, and Lightening Eyes

Now that the braces are gone, the woman in the photo has a couple of blemishes she'd like us to clean up as long as we are here. The Spot Healing Brush is perfect for removing any spots, zits, moles, or other discolorations.

1. Select the Spot Healing Brush and click on any moles or other discolorations to remove them (**Figure 8.9**). Since she had so few, you will need to compare this figure with the previous one to spot what was removed.

2. Most dentists would tell you that her teeth have normal coloring but in this I-want-my-teeth-whiter-than-the-sun era we live in, it isn't white enough. To whiten her teeth select the Dodge tool in the Toolbox (**Figure 8.10**). Make the Option settings Range: Midtones, Exposure: 30%. Change the brush size so it is small enough to paint the teeth without touching the lips.

> **TIP**
>
> If the subject has bloodshot eyes you should use the same technique as used with stained teeth; desaturate the red to gray and then whiten the whites of the eye. If it is serious redness, as caused by conjunctivitis, you may also need to paint some of the area with a small brush at a low opacity.

Figure 8.9
Blemishes are easy to remove with the Spot Healing Brush tool.

3. Paint the teeth just enough to make them slightly brighter as shown in **Figure 8.11**. If the teeth are stained yellow (caused by smoking, coffee, or fluoride in the drinking water), you should first apply the Sponge tool (located next to the Dodge tool) and set the brush to desaturate, which turns the teeth color to gray. After that, brighten them up with the Dodge tool.

Figure 8.10
Using the Dodge tool will help to brighten those teeth.

4. To lighten the eyes, set the Dodge tool to the same settings as we did in Step 2 above, and apply it to the whites of the eyes. Just like the teeth, don't use too much or the subject will appear to be possessed. If you apply the Dodge tool to any other part of the eye it can end up changing the eye color, which may be fun but will detract from the subject. The finished image is shown in **Figure 8.13**.

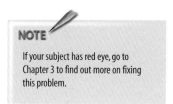

NOTE

If your subject has red eye, go to Chapter 3 to find out more on fixing this problem.

Figure 8.11
After the braces are removed the teeth appear dull.

Figure 8.12
The Dodge tool brightens up her teeth and her smile.

Figure 8.13
After the eyes are lightened the transformation of the photo is complete.

The Spot Healing Brush doesn't require selection of source pixels to operate. Depending on the Type setting, the Spot Healing Brush either uses the pixels around the edge of the selection to find an image area to use as a patch for the selected area (Proximity Match), or uses all the pixels in the selection to create a texture in which to fix the area (Create Texture).

TIP

Use the Healing Brush tool to clean up the appearance of blotchy redness on the skin (see the sidebar, "The Healing Brushes"). You will achieve the best results by using a large brush size. This is because the Healing Brush will blend all the different shades together. Use a Brush size of 50, applying it to the areas with the similar shading.

Body Sculpturing

When people give me a photograph asking me if I can make it look better, they often ask if I can get rid of some pounds. The best answer you can give is a classic smile and say,

"I'll see what I can do." Photoshop Elements is a powerful photo editor, but if someone weighs 400 pounds, there's not much you can do to make them look 300 pounds lighter. Often, the problem isn't extra poundage but terrible camera angle. The photo of the speaker in **Figure 8.14** was taken at a terrible angle, making the speaker look plump.

The most powerful tool in Elements for changing the shape of people or thing is the Liquify Filter. The following exercise demonstrates how you can use this tool to reshape people. This exercise uses the file named **Speaker.jpg** which is available for download on the Peachpit Press Web site.

1. Open the file **Speaker.jpg**. Choose Filter, Distort, Liquify, which opens another dialog that occupies almost the entire screen (**Figure 8.15**).

Figure 8.14
Poor camera angle can produce an unflattering photo.

The Healing Brushes

The Healing Brush first appeared in Photoshop as a godsend for removing scars, blemishes, and all manner of debris. There are two different Healing Brushes in Elements—Spot Healing and Healing. While they are similar in how they work, the results they achieve are quite different. The Healing Brush is used to fix larger areas of imperfections, while the Spot Healing Brush is designed to quickly remove isolated imperfections.

The Healing Brush acts like a smart Clone Stamp tool. You must select a source point for the pixels you want to replace and then paint them over the area that you want to "heal." Unlike the Clone Stamp tool (which just applies the pixels), the Healing Brush blends the new pixels with the existing ones seamlessly.

2. When the file appears in the Liquify workspace, use the Zoom and Hand tools to make the photo fit the screen. Select the Warp tool on the left side of the dialog. Change the Brush size in the Tool Options to 300 pixels. Click and drag the cursor as shown in **Figure 8.16**, next page. As you drag the tool, the shape of the subject changes. You can use Ctrl+Z to undo the last action—but only the last action. To completely reset the image to what it was when the Liquify Filter was opened, you must click the Revert button.

3. When you have finished moving the pixels around, click OK, and the Liquify Filter changes are applied (**Figure 8.17**, next page).

There is much more you can do with the Liquify Filter other than make minor alterations to body shapes. You can do major alterations (**Figure 8.18**, next page) that are just plain silly.

Figure 8.15
The Liquify Filter can distort and reshape almost anything and in the process do a great job of rearranging body shapes.

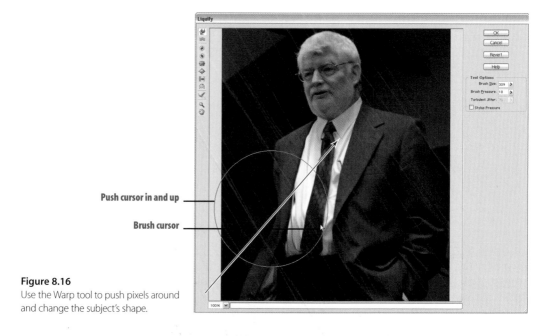

Push cursor in and up ——

Brush cursor ——

Figure 8.16
Use the Warp tool to push pixels around
and change the subject's shape.

Figure 8.17
Using the Liquify Filter allows you to reshape people without making it obvious that you have been altering their
appearance.

Figure 8.18
You can really do some wild and crazy distortions with the
Liquify Filter.

9 Scanning and Repairing Photographs

There is no time like the present when it comes to preserving photographs or any other media. That's because they're not getting any younger—your photographs are aging, and the older they get the less information that can be recovered from the image. Once the photograph has been scanned and stored in the computer, you have stopped the aging process and, as you will learn in this chapter, you can reverse most of the damage done by time and mishandling.

Scanning Photos

Even with a digital camera, you can still use a scanner to capture existing photographs, memorabilia, and important documents like diplomas. Scanning can be accomplished in one of two ways:

- Press the button located on the front of the scanner that launches the scanning software installed onto your computer when you first set up your scanner. Most scanning software will offer you the choice of sending the image to Photoshop Elements, printing it, or saving it as a file.

- Start the scanner directly from Elements by choosing File, Import, and a list of installed imaging devices (cameras and scanners) appears (**Figure 9.1**). Click the scanner in the list and your scanner's user interface (UI) appears (**Figure 9.2**).

NOTE

Windows users may see devices listed with the letters WIA preceding their names. See the sidebar "The Disadvantages of WIA" for more information.

NOTE

The scanner control that appears on your system is determined by the make and model, so it may appear different than the one shown in Figure 9.2.

The Disadvantages of WIA

If your digital camera or scanner is connected to a computer using either Windows XP or Me, each time you attach your camera to the computer, you will be asked what you want the computer to use to talk with your camera. One of those choices will be to move pictures from the camera into the computer using the Windows Imaging Acquisition (WIA) interface. WIA provides a very simple way to move pictures directly from your digital camera (or scanner) to the computer. There is, however, a disadvantage to using the WIA interface. It is a generic, no frills control interface, and therefore not as full-featured as the controls found on the software that comes with your scanner or camera. This is especially true of the WIA interface for your scanner. Many of the features in your scanner that allow you to get the best possible scan are usually not available using the WIA interface.

Figure 9.1
You begin the scanning process from this list of input devices.

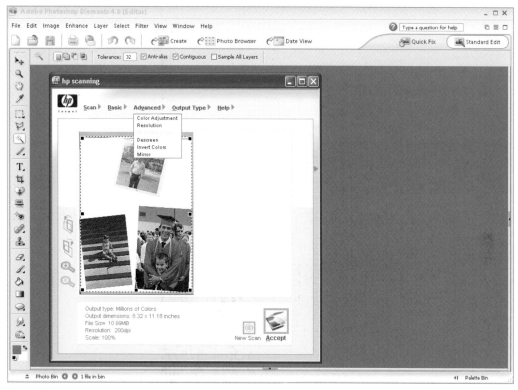

Figure 9.2
The scanner controls appear inside of the Elements workspace.

Basic Scanning in Elements

Here are the four basic steps to follow to scan an image:

1. Preview the image.

2. Select the image.

3. Verify the color mode.

4. Scan the image.

Preview the Image You're Scanning

Most scanner software produces a preview image as soon as the scanner is started. In some cases, the preview scan will not occur immediately because the software is waiting for the lamp in the scanner to warm up, which assures the

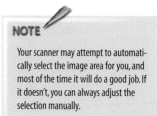

NOTE

Your scanner may attempt to automatically select the image area for you, and most of the time it will do a good job. If it doesn't, you can always adjust the selection manually.

color accuracy of the scan. In rare cases the scanner may be waiting for you to initiate the preview scan.

Preview images are not high quality. They are low-resolution representations of the scanned image used as a guide for selecting the part of the image to be scanned.

Select the Area to be Scanned (Cropping)

Unless instructed otherwise by making a selection, the scanner will scan the entire length of the scanner. You must select the part of the photo you want to scan by clicking over one corner of the image in the preview screen and dragging a selection area over the part of the photo to be scanned (**Figure 9.3**). After you have created a selection you can fine-tune it by moving the selection bars with your mouse. For selecting really small photos, see the section "Selecting Small Images" later in this chapter.

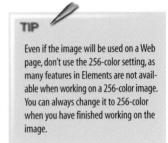

TIP

Even if the image will be used on a Web page, don't use the 256-color setting, as many features in Elements are not available when working on a 256-color image. You can always change it to 256-color when you have finished working on the image.

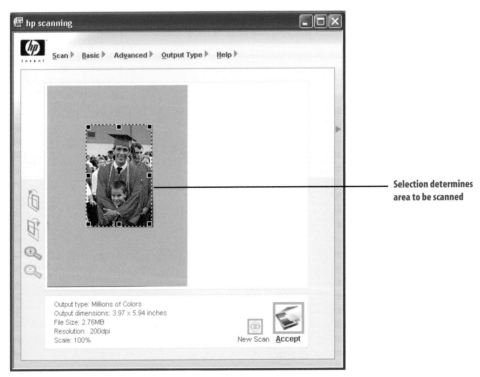

Selection determines area to be scanned

Figure 9.3
Click and drag a selection over the part of the photo to be scanned.

Verify the Color Mode

The scanner may ask you to select the Color Input Mode with choices like Line Art, Halftone, Grayscale, 256-Color, RGB Color, plus all of the possible variations of these modes used by different scanner manufacturers. The scanner software attempts to determine what kind of image you are scanning and set the color mode for you. Since it isn't always correct, you should make sure it is either set to its highest color setting—even if it is a black-and-white document—or to grayscale.

Scanning the Image

The final step is to scan the image, after which the scanner user interface (UI) closes. The scanned image then appears in an image window within Elements (**Figure 9.4**).

TIP

Scanning printed material can create moiré patterns, and some scanners offer a feature that eliminates, or at the least greatly reduces, these patterns. Called de-screening, it typically must be selected from a tool bar in the scanning software user interface (UI). After selecting it the scanner will rescan the preview. The speed of the Preview mode is much slower than normal preview.

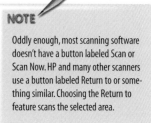

NOTE

Oddly enough, most scanning software doesn't have a button labeled Scan or Scan Now. HP and many other scanners use a button labeled Return to or something similar. Choosing the Return to feature scans the selected area.

Figure 9.4
The scanned image appears in an image window in Elements.

Cool Things You Can Do Using Your Scanner and Photoshop Elements

The previous section covered the basics of scanning in a photo; now we'll look at some other feats your scanner can perform that you may not know about.

Accurately Select Small Images or Areas

If you are selecting a single item out of many on a sheet of paper, or if you are scanning a very small original, or if the selection of the area to be scanned is critical, here is how to make an accurate selection.

1. On the preview screen for your scan, click and drag a rectangle of the area that you want to scan. After you have made a rough selection (**Figure 9.5**), you can move the selection bars by clicking and dragging them to the desired position.

Figure 9.5
Begin by making a rough selection.

2. After you have made the first selection, locate the button or command that allows you to zoom in on the selected area. On the HP Precisionscan Pro dialog (**Figure 9.6**), it is the magnifying glass button. When enabled, the scanner will scan the image again, and the selected area will fill the preview window. Now that the preview scan fills the screen area, you can make any critical adjustments to the selection bars and also see if you need to clean your scanner copy glass.

TIP

If the photo isn't oriented correctly, you can rotate it at this point using the scanning software or scan it into the computer and rotate it using the Straightening tool in Photoshop Elements.

Zoom button   **Accept button starts the scan**

Figure 9.6
Zooming in fills the preview window with the scanned image.

Enlarge Photos with Your Scanner

One of the great features of a scanner that is rarely used is its ability to change the size of an image. The size of an image can be enlarged in Photoshop Elements through a process called *resampling*. No matter how good Elements is, when you increase the size of a photo through resampling, the image is visibly degraded—it loses sharpness and detail. If the same photo is scaled by the scanner when it is scanned, it can be made several times larger without the accompanying loss of detail (see **Figures 9.7** and **9.8**).

The scanning software assumes you want to scan the image at 100%—the final size is the same as the original. Every manufacturer's scanning software controls the size of the resulting scan from different locations. In most HP scanners, it is found in the Tools menu, and is called Resize.

NOTE

If the original photo is of poor quality, the enlarged image will also be poor quality, and as a result of being larger, the defects will be more apparent.

Figure 9.7
The original photo was quite small.

Figure 9.8
The scanner achieved the best possible enlargement and Elements corrected the color shift produced by aging.

Scanning Multiple Images

If you have ever scanned a lot of photos on a flatbed scanner, you know that it can be quite a process. Each photo must be accurately placed on the scanner glass, previewed, scanned, removed from the scanner glass, and then the process is repeated.

With Elements, you can place as many photos as will fit on the scanner glass, scan them all at once, and then let Elements sort them out for you. Here is how it works:

1. Place the photos on the scanner glass in any order or orientation and choose File > Import, and select your scanner, which then makes a preview scan.

2. Create a selection that includes all of the photos, as shown in **Figure 9.9**, next page and scan the image.

3. Choose Image, Divide Scanned Photos (**Figure 9.10**, next page). Elements begins to straighten and separate each photo and place it in its own image window, as shown in **Figure 9.11** (page 237). That's all there is to it. All that remains is to name and save each image.

TIP

The Divide Scanned Photos command can also be used to straighten and crop a single image on the scanner, which can be a real time-saver.

Figure 9.9
Select all the photos on the scanner.

Figure 9.10
The Divide Scanned Photos command.

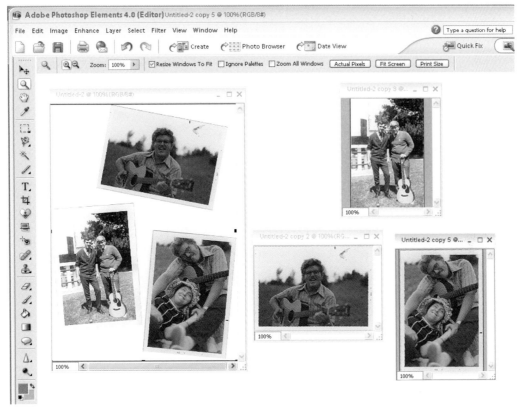

Figure 9.11
Elements automatically separated, cropped, and placed each photo in its own image window.

Preparing to Restore Photos

If you are scanning an image for the purpose of restoring it, you will need to make a few adjustments to the normal scanning routine we have been learning.

If you are scanning a photo or other document to repair it, follow these scanning guidelines. They differ from normal scanning in several ways.

TIP

If the photo or image that you are scanning is old and fragile, you should exercise caution when handling and preparing it for scanning.

Enlarge the Original

Make it a general rule to scan images that are to be repaired, or otherwise restored, at twice the original size. By doubling the size of the original, you are forcing the scanner to capture the maximum amount of detail in the original photo and you are giving yourself more material to work with. There are some exceptions to this rule: When the original is really small, you should consider using an even larger resize factor (like 300%–500%). Also, if the original image is so huge that it covers the entire scanner glass, then 100% will probably be sufficient.

When you have completed the restoration, resize the image to return it to its correct size, which produces a natural softening that is the result of making it smaller. This can sometimes make a harsh image look better. If it softens it too much, use an application of the Unsharp Mask Filter (Filter, Sharpen, Unsharp Mask) at a low setting.

Use the Highest Quality Scan Setting

In short, you want to get the maximum amount of image detail from the scanned image as is possible, with little to no concern about how big the final file will be. For photos and memorabilia that you want to preserve, scan the original as RGB (24-bit) color. Black-and-white photos in most cases should be scanned as grayscale, the exception being if they have been hand-colored, or have a colored stain on them. Preserving the color in such cases allows isolation of the stain using color-sensitive selection tools.

Store Using a Lossless File Format

Do not save the original as a JPEG file. For restoration work, you should not save the images you are working on using any file format that uses lossy file compression. This includes Wavelet, JPEG, and JPEG 2000. Lossy file compression degrades the image. Probably the most popular graphic format to use is TIFF (Tagged Image File Format), and you can choose one of several compression options that are lossless, meaning they do not degrade the image. Be careful not to choose the JPEG compression option, which is now available as a choice for TIFF.

General Print Handling Procedures and Precautions

Here are some points to consider when handling prints, slides, and negatives:

- Always hold prints or negatives by their edges. Do not touch the surface if you're not wearing cotton gloves; even clean fingers can leave natural secretions that can damage a photo over time. You can purchase cotton gloves specially made for handling photos at your local camera store.

- Don't mark the back of your photo permanently in any way. The chemicals in some markers (especially a Sharpie) will eventually find their way to the other side of the photograph and ruin it. If you must make a temporary identification, write brief information gently with only a very soft 2B or 4B pencil.

- Never repair a photograph by applying adhesive tape to it. I saw the Dead Sea scrolls exhibit and after talking to one of the archivists, I discovered that one of the major restoration tasks they have been doing for the past five years was removing the Scotch tape that the original curators used to piece it together. If you have a photo that is in several pieces, keep all of the pieces in a clean, chemically inert polyester bag or sleeves.

Repairing Tears and Creases

One of more common problems with old photos is that they usually have not received museum-quality care and storage. Unprotected, important images can easily become bent, folded, and otherwise damaged. Physically, there isn't anything that can be done for the original (with the exception of work done by a restoration specialist), but it's relatively easy to repair an electronic version and then to print it.

The damage caused by folding a photograph depends on its age and the material it is printed on. Photos taken in the past decade are printed on a flexible Mylar that can stand almost any degree of contortion, while photos printed in the early 20th century were printed on stiff material, and in most cases even a slight bend produces a hard, raised crease from which the image surface may flake off, like the example shown in **Figure 9.12**.

Figure 9.12
Creases and tears are a common form of damage found in old photos.

The Power of the Healing and Spot Healing Brushes

Before Adobe introduced the Healing brushes back in Elements 3, repairing a crease like that in **Figure 9.12** required using the Clone Stamp tool. Typically it took quite an effort to make the repair and not leave any sign of previous damage. Elements now has two tools, the Healing Brush and the Spot Healing Brush, which make the repair of image defects much easier.

How the Healing Brush Works

The **Healing Brush**, inherited from Adobe Photoshop and located in the Toolbox, is a brush that is similar in operation to the Clone Stamp tool in that it takes samples from one part of an image and paints them onto another. Selection of the source pixels is accomplished by Alt-clicking on a source area.

What makes the Healing Brush different from the Clone Stamp tool is what happens after the pixels are applied. The Healing Brush blends the texture and color from the sample area with the pixels where the brush is applied. You can actually see the blending happening after applying the brush.

The **Spot Healing Brush** uses pixels from another part of the image: it produces a selection, evaluates the surrounding pixels, and then blends them before removing the selection.

Removing a Crease or Tear

I have scanned a photo that was taken over 100 years ago on which you can practice using the Healing Brush and Spot Healing Brush. Here is the step-by-step procedure:

1. Download the photo **Bearded_man.jpg** from the Peachpit Press Web site and open it.

2. Select the Healing Brush tool (J). Right-click to open a separate Brush Settings dialog. Change the brush setting to a 30 px brush with a Hardness of 0% (**Figure 9.13**). We are using a brush wide enough to cover the entire width of the crease. In the Options bar ensure that Source is Sampled and Aligned is checked.

3. Place the Healing Brush tool on the spot shown in **Figure 9.14** (page 242) and Alt-click the brush to establish the source point. Next, click (don't drag) the brush one time at the point on the crease indicated in Figure 9.13. The crease underneath the brush, where you applied the Healing Brush, disappears.

4. Hold down the Shift key and click at a point at the top of the crease shown in **Figure 9.15** (page 242). The entire crease disappears. What happened? The Healing Brush tool painted a straight line from the first click made in the previous step to the second click just made.

Healing Brush   Sampled   Aligned   Set to 30   Set to zero

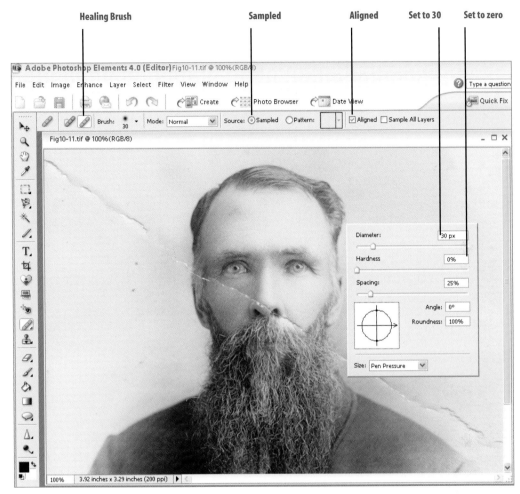

Figure 9.13
Select a brush size that is wider than the crease being repaired.

5. Use the Zoom tool (Z) to zoom in close enough so the left side of the subject's face fills the display (**Figure 9.16**). When working on areas that have detailed information, I don't recommend using the automatic Shift key feature because it will produce a visibly brighter area. When restoring the damage on the cheek, try picking a source point below the damage. When working on the nose, and on the hair, a point above the damage appears to work best. We're done with the Healing Brush.

TIP

When working in areas of high contrast use the Clone Stamp tool instead of the Healing or Spot Healing Brush tools.

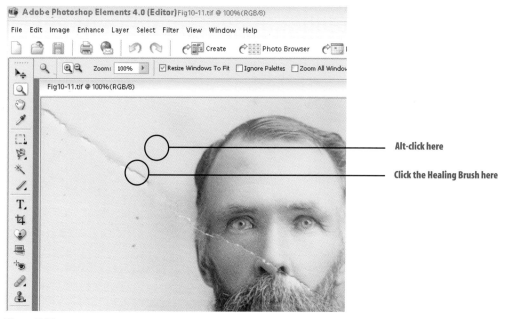

Figure 9.14
Select a clean point near the crease as source pixels before clicking the Healing Brush tool on the crease.

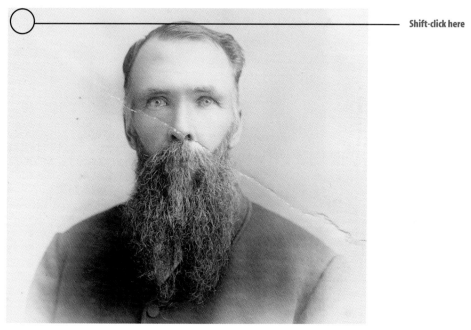

Figure 9.15
Smaller brush sizes produce better results.

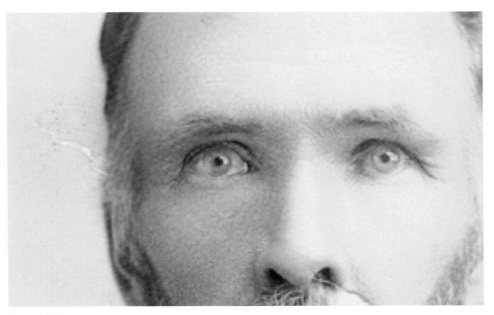

Figure 9.16
The Healing Brush is also used to repair the cheek and nose areas of the photo.

6. There isn't a good source area for the dark area in the nostril (ugh), so we'll switch to the Spot Healing Brush (which doesn't require a source point). In the Options bar, set the brush size to 6 pixels and click (don't drag) on the damaged area. This brush works best when used with small brush sizes and on isolated areas of damage or debris.

7. Use the Spot Healing brush to remove the remaining parts of the crease near the head and some of the dark spots on the background. Be careful not to apply the tool to areas that are too close to adjacent areas that are either much darker or much brighter than the area you are fixing. The Spot Healing Brush uses those pixels when calculating the blend, and if their shading differs greatly from the area you're working on, a noticeable smudge will result.

TIP

A quick way to move between the Healing Brush and the Spot Healing Brush is to press Shift and the J key. This is true of all tools that are grouped together. If you want to toggle between tools without having to use the Shift key, go to Edit, Preferences, General and uncheck Use Shift Key for Tool Switch.

8. Return to Actual Pixels (Alt+Ctrl+0) to see how the restoration appears (**Figure 9.17**, next page).

Figure 9.17
The damage to the photograph has been removed, and the digital image is immune to further aging.

Fixing Other Photo Problems

While fixing antique photos is fun, a more common problem is working with color photos taken in the last 40 years. Even if not exposed to daylight, the dyes in the photos are changing color. In the next exercise, we'll color-correct an image and learn a different way to remove damage and debris. This exercise uses the file **Guitar_man.jpg**, which is available from the Peachpit Press Web site.

1. Open the file **Guitar_man.jpg** (**Figure 9.18**). The photo was taken in the early '70s, so there are several things that need attention. The colors are shifting with age (moving toward magenta), and something is splattered on the photo. We'll tackle the splatter first.

2. Select the Rectangular Marquee tool (M) in the Toolbox. In the Options bar, change the Feather value to 3 pixels. Click in the image and drag a rectangle selection over a section of the background that is relatively free from defects (**Figure 9.19**). Size and location are not critical.

3. Select the Move tool (V). Hold down the Alt key. Click the cursor inside the selection and drag it across the photo until it is on top of the debris (**Figure 9.20**, page 246), and then let go of the mouse button. The selection becomes a floating selection containing a copy of the pixels that it originally surrounded. When the mouse button is released the pixels in the selection replace the pixels below it.

Figure 9.18
There is junk splattered on the photo, and the colors are shifting with age.

Figure 9.19
Create a selection over a clean area of the background.

Figure 9.20
Dragging a floating selection partially covers the debris on the photo.

4. With the Alt key still held down, drag the selection up until it covers the remainder of the debris and release the mouse button again. As long as the Alt key is held down when you move the selection, a copy of the originally selected pixels moves with it.

5. When you are rid of the debris in the sky, Ctrl+D removes the floating selection. Continue to drag the floating selection until all of the debris has been covered up.

6. Correcting the color shift in photos like these is quite simple. Choose Enhance, Auto Color Correction (Shift+Ctrl+B). The color shift is almost completely removed (**Figure 9.21**).

7. The photo is still too dark, so apply Shadows/Highlights (Enhance, Adjust Lighting, Shadows/Highlights). The filter automatically increases the brightness of the shadows, but this photo is backlit, so increase the Lighten Shadows slider up to 40% (**Figure 9.22**).

8. Use the Spot Healing Brush to remove the debris around the head. Apply Smart Auto Fix (Ctrl+M) to balance out the darker areas. At this point the image will appear a little noisy so apply the Reduce Noise Filter (Filter, Noise, Reduce Noise) at the default settings.

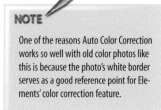

NOTE

One of the reasons Auto Color Correction works so well with old color photos like this is because the photo's white border serves as a good reference point for Elements' color correction feature.

Figure 9.21
The Auto Color Correction removes the color shift caused by aging.

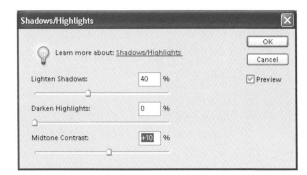

Figure 9.22
The Shadows/Highlights command increases the brightness of the shadow region without affecting the brighter areas.

9. The color is still not quite right, so we need to use the Adjust Color for Skin Tone feature (see **Figure 9.23**, next page). This tool is new in Photoshop Elements 4. It is located in the Enhance, Color Adjust menu. Just click somewhere on the guitar player's face and almost immediately the colors are almost perfect. The borders of the photo are no longer white, so use the Rectangle Marquee tool to select the area inside the border of the print, and then reverse the selection (Ctrl+Shift+I) and fill in the border with white (see **Figure 9.24**, next page). You're done.

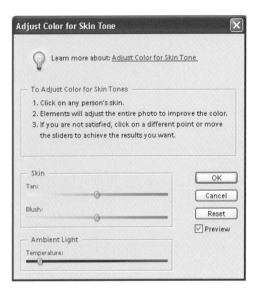

Figure 9.23
Adjust Color for Skin Tone corrects the colors in the photos based on the skin tone of the subject.

Figure 9.24
After performing some final cleanup tasks the photo is once again ready for primetime.

We have covered some of the basics of scanning and photo restoration in this chapter. It is so much fun to restore old photos and not-so-old photos to see what things used to look like. In the next chapter, we'll really kick out the stops and learn how to create stunning panoramas with Elements.

10 Creating Stunning Panoramas

Before I began using Photoshop Elements, I had limited experience creating panoramas. This was because making them without using a program specifically designed to create them was a major effort. After using Photoshop Elements' Photomerge feature, however, I was hooked. One of the challenges for me in writing this chapter was to remember that not everyone makes panoramas or photo montages. So I promise not to get too carried away—maybe. But after you read this chapter, you might get inspired!

The Power of the Panorama

Panoramas are not a new thing. Soon after the invention of photography in 1839, the desire to show the broad expanse of both cities and landscapes—or large groups of people—prompted photographers to begin creating panoramas (**Figure 10.1** is a panorama of a Texas oil field near Houston that was taken in 1919.). Sadly most of the early panoramas no longer exist. The U.S. Library of Congress maintains a very large collection of panoramas that can be viewed online at http://memory.loc.gov/ammem/collections/panoramic_photo/.

Figure 10.1
This early panorama was photographed in 1919.

Say the word *panorama* and most people envision a wide, full-color photograph of some majestic landscape, such as the Grand Canyon, or a tropical paradise. But panoramas have most often been used to document people, places, and events. Pictures of high school graduation classes are often captured using specialized (and expensive) panorama cameras, which were the only way to produce a panorama before digital photo editing came along. Today, any camera can take the picture elements required to build a panorama—with a little help from Photoshop Elements.

Taking Pictures for a Panorama

Of all the features and projects that can be accomplished by using Photoshop Elements, making a good panorama is unique in that it requires preparation on the photographic side. Taking photos to be used in a panorama isn't *that* hard—it just takes some getting used to.

What You Need to Take Panorama Photos

Many digital cameras have a panorama assist mode, which allows you to take multiple shots of wide scenes that you can later stitch together with the Photomerge feature in Elements. Photomerge is very effective at seamlessly stitching the separate photos together.

Typically when a camera is set to panorama mode you take the first shot, then pan the camera in the selected direction. About a third of the shot appears as a semi-transparent image on the LCD (**Figure 10.2**). For each subsequent shot, you superimpose the image to match the next part of the scene.

Exposure and white balance are locked when you take the first photo so the same settings are used for each subsequent shot in the series.

Figure 10.2.
The panorama mode of your digital camera assists in making shots that make seamless panoramas.

Following are a couple of rules and general guidelines that might help you take good panorama photos.

Stabilize Your Camera

Whether your camera has a panorama assist mode or you are shooting manually, you should use a tripod when taking panorama photos, as it is easier to overlap each photo. If you don't have your tripod with you there are alternative ways to stabilize your camera. Look for a flat horizontal surface like a fence post, a rock, or even the hood of your car. When the surface is uneven, you can use something soft like clothing or a bean bag to set the camera on to help maintain the camera level while shooting. That said, some of my best panoramic shots were taken without using a tripod; the resulting panoramas came out because of my using a tripod substitute, or just by dumb luck.

Consider Your Light Source

The second thing necessary for creating a great panorama is having the sun or other light source behind or above you, rather than at one end of the scene or the other. An exception to this rule is sunrise and sunset photos. The goal is to prevent the individual photos used to make the panorama from having different levels of brightness that result in light and dark lines of demarcation in the final image or as lighter spots, as shown in **Figure 10.3**. This panorama was created from three photos. The center photo was lighter than the other two. When Photomerge merged the photos, it attempted to blend the edges, resulting in the unique area of light in the middle.

Bright spots caused by mismatch of panels.

Figure 10.3
If the separate photos have different overall brightness, it can produce dark or light areas in the panorama.

Don't Get Too Close

When taking panoramic pictures, you want to get as far away from the subject as is reasonable. The closer you are to the subject, the wider the setting on your zoom lens; this produces greater barrel distortion on each photo. If there's too much distortion, even Photomerge cannot prevent weird-looking gaps between each panel, like the image shown in **Figure 10.4**. So get a good distance away from your subject when possible.

Figure 10.4
Taking photos too close to the subject often results in a panorama that looks like Picasso created it.

Controlling Overlap

Panoramas are made by stitching several photos together using the Photomerge Panorama command. To make a panorama that appears seamless, it is necessary for there to be some amount of overlap between each photo—just enough to get the job done. With too much overlap, the panorama file becomes huge and the program often has trouble stitching the photos together. How much overlap is enough? For this program thirty percent overlap is about right.

So, if your camera doesn't have a panorama assist mode how do you measure a thirty percent overlap? Here is a trick that I use. When I take the initial photograph, I note some point of reference in the LCD frame of my digital camera. As I rotate the camera (more on that in a moment), I try to make sure that the reference point remains in the right or left third of the frame (depending on which way I turn it).

If you aren't using a tripod, when you turn the camera, make every effort to have the camera lens rotate around an imaginary axis. When I first started taking panoramic photos, I held the camera and turned my body. By doing that, I changed the angle of the camera in reference to the scenery that I was photographing. It is less important when the subject is a great distance away, but it becomes important when the subject matter is close.

We cover additional tips later in this chapter. Now it's time to make a simple panorama.

Creating a Simple Panorama

For the first panorama, let's make a simple one from three photos. If you downloaded the files for this chapter, we will be using **Ship_Left.jpg, Ship_Middle.jpg** and **Ship_Right.jpg**.

1. Choose File, New, Photomerge Panorama. The dialog that appears allows you to select the photos used in the panorama (**Figure 10.5**) with the Browse button. If any photos are already open in Photoshop Elements, they appear on this list. Photomerge lists the order of the files in alphabetical order and this order has no affect on the order of assembly in the panorama. Click OK.

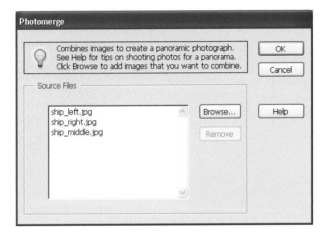

Figure 10.5
The images to be included in the panorama are selected from the Photomerge dialog.

2. Photomerge works on the image for a few moments. How long this takes is a function of the size and number of the photos and the horsepower of your system. If Photomerge can't figure out how to assemble the photos, a message is displayed telling you to manually align the photos (**Figure 10.6**). If this happens, just click and drag the thumbnails into the workspace and put the photos in the correct order. Use the Navigator on the right side of the dialog to zoom in and fill the screen with the panorama (**Figure 10.7**). After you have the photos in the correct order, go to the next step, but don't click the OK button yet.

Figure 10.6
If Photomerge cannot automatically determine the correct order of the photos, it asks you to put them in the right order.

Figure 10.7
Use the Photomerge control dialog to edit the panorama.

3. No panorama matches perfectly. Look carefully at the top and bottom edge of the image **(Figure 10.8**, next page), and you can see that the pieces don't exactly match up. Why? The camera was handheld and the orientation of the camera changed slightly between photos. Slight mismatches like this are common and can be left alone and the process of making the panorama usually flattens them out **(Figure 10.9**, next page). Now click OK and Photomerge will grind away for a few minutes before producing the panorama.

4. To finish up, flatten the panorama (select Layers, Flatten Image), and select the Crop tool (C) to remove parts of the image that are not required **(Figure 10.10**, next page).

Figure 10.8
Using the default setting causes there to be mismatch at the edge.

Figure 10.9
Photomerge seamlessly (almost) made the three photos into a single image.

Figure 10.10
A simple panorama made by using Photomerge and three photographs.

Creating a Panorama from Two Photos

Since aligning edges is something that will always be part of making panoramas, the next exercise uses only two photos, and will let you see more features. If you want to try your hand at this, the files have been made available for download on the Peachpit Press Web page:

1. From the Create Photomerge dialog select **Bomber_left.jpg** and **Bomber_right.jpg**. Use the Browse button to locate the two files and click OK. The photos will probably stitch together in the correct order. If not, click and drag them into the correct order.

2. When the stitched image appears in the Photomerge dialog, it is apparent there is an alignment problem (**Figure 10.11**) with the image. The first problem is misalignment. Both the propeller and the ladder underneath the plane are misaligned. Unlike the first exercise, this misalignment will be very visible. The Perspective button can be used to correct the misalignment. Select the right panel (it will become highlighted in red) and click the Perspective button. The right side of the aircraft becomes very large and so do the kids under the wing (**Figure 10.12**, next page).

Figure 10.11
This panorama, made by using two photos, has an alignment problem to overcome.

Figure 10.12
The Perspective feature corrects the misalignment but distorts the wing and the people in the scene.

3. If the right panel is not enlarged select the Set Vanishing Point Tool (V) and click on the left panel. When working with two panels, you can decide which one becomes distorted using the Set Vanishing Point tool. In this case, the plane looks better if the right panel is selected because it keeps the people in the photograph of normal size. While it distorts the size of the aircraft nose, that looks fine with the nose art and all of the machine guns (**Figure 10.13**). Using Perspective corrects the misalignment perfectly. If you are thinking the propeller over the cockpit has a slight misalignment, you are actually seeing the edge of the canopy.

The Unique Way Photomerge Stitches Photos

When you looked at Figure 10.12 you may have wondered why the light or darker areas appear as a diagonal line when the photos were stitched together, rather than a vertical line running along the edge of the photo. This is because Photomerge stitches photos together along a diagonal line rather than the vertical line that naturally exists between the photos. It seems that it is done this way to reduce the appearance of any hints of lines by spreading them across the diagonal.

64.57%   4.56 inches x 2.757 inches (300 ppi)

Figure 10.13
Changing the vanishing point changes which panel is distorted to correct the misalignment.

4. Even though these photos were taken within seconds of one another, there is a noticeable shading difference, as shown in **Figure 10.14**, next page. To correct this, select the Advanced Blending option. A preview of the blended image appears (**Figure 10.15**). The before and after is shown in **Figure 10.16** (page 261). Click Exit Preview and then click OK. After a few moments, Elements creates the initial panorama.

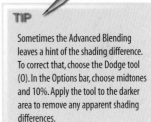

TIP

Sometimes the Advanced Blending leaves a hint of the shading difference. To correct that, choose the Dodge tool (O). In the Options bar, choose midtones and 10%. Apply the tool to the darker area to remove any apparent shading differences.

Figure 10.14
The difference in shading in these photos is apparent.

Figure 10.15
After Advanced Blending is applied, the difference in shading is no longer noticeable.

Figure 10.16
Before Advanced Blending was applied. After Advanced Blending was applied.

5. Several things remain to be done. First, from the Layer menu, choose Flatten Image. Next, crop the image using the Crop tool (C).

6. This next part is optional but I used the Clone Stamp Tool to remove the ladder from under the plane (**Figure 10.17**).

That completes the panorama and it only took a few minutes.

Figure 10.17
After you flatten and crop, the panorama looks pretty good.

Making Very Wide Panoramas

A question that often arises is: What is the maximum width that a panorama can be? There is no exact answer to that question because as you continue to take photos and rotate your body, you will eventually turn a full 360° and begin covering the same area again. When you make really wide panoramas, the presentation of the composition becomes a problem. One concern of a really wide composition has to do with the aspect ratio of the final image. As you continue to add images and make the image wider, the height remains the same. The following figures provide a visual example of this diminishing ratio. The subject of this panorama was a fantastic mural painted on a construction site fence in downtown St. Louis. It took seven photographs to capture all of it. If we make a mural from only two panels **(Figure 10.18)** the image is 4 by 1.75 inches. Add two more panels to the panorama **(Figure 10.19)** and its width expands to 7.4 inches but its height remains at 1.75 inches. By the time all of the panels are included another phenomenon becomes apparent. The mural is almost the width of a city block so while the center portions of the mural are less than 15 feet from the camera, the ends of the murals are over 50 feet and therefore they appear much smaller than the fence in the center. **(Figure 10.20)**.

Figure 10.18
A panorama made with two photo has an acceptable aspect ratio.

Figure 10.19
When the number of photos increases to four the composition is becoming wider but not taller.

Figure 10.20
With all seven photos used both end pieces are so far from the camera they appear smaller.

One solution is to use the Perspective tool, which was used to correct the misalignment in the previous exercise **(Figure 10.21)**. Because it is composed of an odd number of photo panels, Photomerge correctly selects the vanishing point. If there is an even number of panels, the program doesn't know which part is the center. Selecting an edge panel as the vanishing point creates extreme distortion at the opposite end of the panorama and is not recommended.

Figure 10.21
Using the Perspective makes the ends distorted but now all of the panels are nearly the same size.

Getting Creative

Just because the subject is wide does not mean that the resulting panorama has to be wide too. The Photomerge feature lets you move and stack the images in any fashion you desire. One example is to put three panels on top and four on the bottom **(Figure 10.22)** You can also use Photomerge to make a collage of many different images; at the points where the photos overlap, the program will merge them **(Figure 10.23**, next page). You can then combine the two compositions together. In the example shown **(Figure 10.24**, next page), the background was colorized (Ctrl+U) and faded using the Lightness slider, and then the mural composition was rotated (Ctrl+T). Then, to complete the work, text was added and the Wow Neon Red style was applied.

Figure 10.22
There is no law that says all of the panels must be placed end to end—be creative.

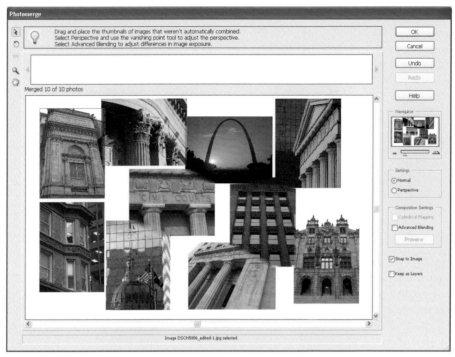

Figure 10.23
Photomerge can also be used to create a montage using multiple unrelated photographs.

Figure 10.24
This montage was composed of two works created in Photomerge.

Vertical Panoramas

Not all panoramas are wide. Photomerge has the ability to make vertical as well as horizontal panoramas. There are a lot of things in this world that are taller than they are wide—Michael Jordan comes to mind. The panorama in **Figure 10.25** was made from three photographs. In Photomerge, all that was necessary to arrange them into a vertical format was to drag each image on top of the other. The challenge faced when using vertical panoramas is that they can be difficult to lay out in a publication (like this book).

Multiple Panels Overlaid

As shown with the Saint Louis mural, photos in a panorama do not need to line up neat and tidy in a row. Here is another idea for a different type of panorama. This technique works best when the photos have been taken with the thought of creating a panorama. In this example, four photographs are lined up horizontally but instead of overlapping the entire edge, each photo is rotated and only one corner of the edges overlap each other **(Figure 10.26**, next page). Rotating images inside of the Photomerge dialog requires selecting the image and then choosing the Rotate tool, positioning it on a corner of the selected image, and rotating it. To move to the next image requires reselecting the Move tool, selecting the next image, and then rotating it. In the finished composition **(Figure 10.27**, next page) a Drop Shadow Layer Style is applied to the layer before it is finally flattened.

Figure 10.25
Not all panoramas have to be horizontal.

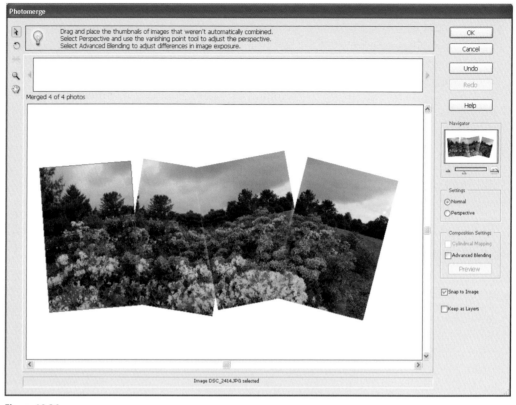

Figure 10.26
This panorama involves rotating the images so only a small portion overlaps.

Figure 10.27
The montage created by Photomerge has a drop shadow effect applied to it.

The challenge I had with the waterfall on the Bull Creek panorama (**Figure 10.28**) was that diffused light from the overcast sky had made the falls dark. The solution was to take two sets of panoramic photos. I shot the first set using the sky as the light source. The second set of photos I took by using the spot setting on my camera, so that the exposure would be adjusted correctly for the waterfall portion, even though the sky would be overexposed (washed out). I created two separate panoramas from the photos, and then merged the two panoramas using layers in Elements. To learn more about using layers see Chapter 6.

Figure 10.28
This photo was made from two sets of photos taken at two different exposure settings.

How to Print Panoramas

Because I like to print my panoramas, I make sure that the width is 20 inches or less. The trick with printing panoramas is to have a printer that can print either on panorama-sized paper or on roll paper. This typically means that the preferred printer accepts paper from the rear. Since every HP printer I have ever worked with feeds paper from the front, with few exceptions, they cannot be used to print panoramas.

TIP

If your panorama is larger than the paper you are printing on, you should resize the image using your photo-editing software. Do not let the printer software do it because the quality of the resized image will not be as good.

Epson offers panorama paper in a single, fixed size, but if you use this paper you must make sure that your panorama fits the paper you are using. If you are using roll paper, then theoretically you can make your panoramas any size you want. However, when you want to frame your panorama, you will discover that panorama frames are not common—and that custom frames are expensive.

I could write another 30 pages on this subject, but I have it on good authority that most of the readers are not as interested (read: obsessed) with panoramas as I am. But maybe this chapter has given you the bug…

11 Sharing Your Photos

Once you have sorted, organized, and fixed all of your photos, the next logical step is to share these photographic masterpieces with others. Back in the days of film, the only way to share your favorite photos was to make multiple prints and mail them to others, or gather your friends together in your home and have them watch a slide show. The latter event was often considered torture for the viewers. With Photoshop Elements, you have many more choices. In this chapter, you will learn how to make a wide variety of cool creations both printed and electronic. We'll begin by learning how to use Elements and your printer to create stunning photographs that look as good, or even better, than what you would get from your local one-hour photo service.

Making Great Photos on Your Printer

Printing from Elements, as with any other program, is easy. Just select the Print command and your prints come out of your photo printer. But, regardless of how good you make your photographs look on the computer, if you cannot get good-quality prints from your printer, it can be frustrating. If you've ever printed something using Adobe Photoshop, you will remember being faced with a bewildering selection of features and options from which to pick. You'll be relieved to learn that Elements has really streamlined the printing process.

In this chapter, you'll learn how to make all kinds of cool picture packages with the click of a button. Also, you'll learn how to make great photos on almost any inkjet printer. Finally, you'll discover some of the options available to you for making hard copies of your masterpieces.

Basic Photo Printing

Basic printing using Elements is a two-step process:

- **Preview Size and Orientation**. This ensures the photo is the right size and orientation.

- **Print**. This controls printer selection and provides access to printer properties.

While printing with Elements is really simple, I have included the following step-by-step exercises so that you can see how the different parts of the print dialogs interact with one another.

1. Select the Select Print option from the File menu (Ctrl+P), and when the Print Preview dialog opens (see **Figure 11.1**), you can see that the photo appears very small in the Preview window. The size of the image that appears in the Preview window reflects the paper size setting of the selected printer. For example, in Figure 11.1 the selected printer is currently set to use letter-size paper.

2. The settings on the right (Print Size and Scaled Print Size) control the size of the printed image and both functionally do the same thing. The Print Size setting contains a short list of standard print sizes in addition to Fit On Page and Custom Size. The Custom Size setting appears if you manually enter in a new size using the Scaled Print Size. Change the Print Size and

NOTE

You can't change the printer paper size from this dialog. See the section "When the Photo Doesn't Fit" for details on changing paper size.

TIP

If your photo is not oriented correctly, click the rotate icons located below the preview (**Figure 11.2**).

TIP

Ensure that the Center Image in the Position section is always checked to make sure your photo ends up in the center of the paper.

the size of the preview changes. A warning may appear (**Figure 11.3**, next page) letting you know if you are enlarging a photo too much, causing its resolution to drop below 220 dpi, meaning it will print a poorer quality photo.

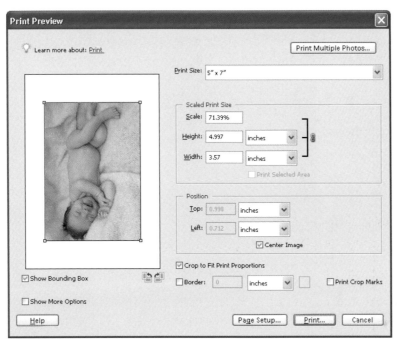

Figure 11.1
Check to make sure that photo orientation and size are correct before pressing the Print button.

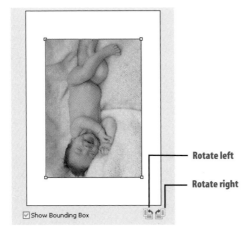

Figure 11.2
Changing a photo's orientation on the page is accomplished using these icons.

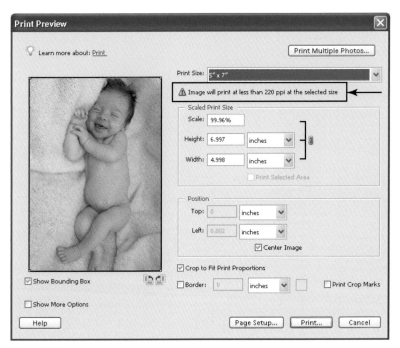

Figure 11.3
A warning appears when the resolution of the enlarged photo gets too low.

Previewing Your Print Job

If you're a novice to printing photos, use the Print Preview feature to make sure that what you are about to print will be the size that you are expecting. For example, when you are working on a photo in Elements the photograph might fill the screen. Only when the photo is previewed in the Print Preview dialog does its true printed size become apparent.

When the Photo Doesn't Fit

If the photo in the Preview area doesn't fit, there are several possible reasons: the paper size is too small or the image is too large. If the paper size selected by the printer is too small, do the following:

1. Click the Page Setup button. This opens the Page Setup dialog.

2. Select a larger Paper Size setting (**Figure 11.4**). If the paper size you want isn't on the list, it may be because the currently selected printer doesn't support it. You can't tell which printer is currently selected from this dialog either.

Figure 11.4
Choose Page Setup to change
the paper size.

If the paper size is the correct size, the image itself may be too large—see the sidebar "Image Size Vs. Resolution." You can make Elements resize the image by choosing one of the preset sizes back in the Print Preview.

What happens when the image appears to be the size of a postage stamp (**Figure 11.5**, next page)? This is usually caused by the resolution of the image being set too high. You can change the size of the photo in the Print Preview, but I recommend that you exit Print Preview and change the size in the Elements Editor using Image, Resize, Image Size.

Image Size Vs. Resolution

How can an image that is 4 by 3 inches at the same time be 18 by 13 inches? The answer is resolution. At a resolution of 300 dots per inch (dpi) the image will print out at approximately 4 by 3 inches. If the resolution is changed to 72 dpi the same photo would print at 18 by 13 inches. The quality of the larger image would be much poorer due to the lower resolution. While everyone has a different opinion about what is minimum resolution for a good print, Adobe says that photos with less than 220 dpi make poorer prints and I find that 150 dpi produces an acceptable quality print. You are the final judge for what is and is not an acceptable quality level for your photos.

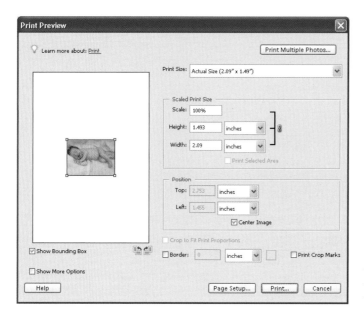

Figure 11.5
When the resolution is too high the image preview reveals a very tiny photo.

Where is the Printer?

Checking which printer is selected and how that printer is set up from within Elements can be done in two ways—from the Print Preview dialog (File, Print) or the Page Setup dialog (File, Page Setup) as appears in **Figure 11.6**.

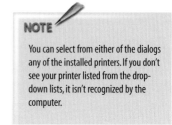

NOTE

You can select from either of the dialogs any of the installed printers. If you don't see your printer listed from the drop-down lists, it isn't recognized by the computer.

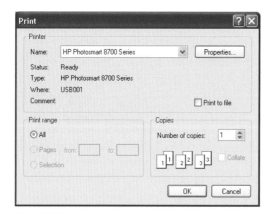

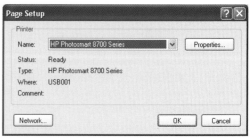

Figure 11.6
Two different ways (Print and Page Setup) to choose and configure a printer.

Setting Up Your Printer

Once you have selected the printer, the next step is to set it up. This is done by clicking the Properties button on the upper-right corner of the Print or Page Setup dialog. The Printer Properties dialog appears (**Figures 11.7**). Each dialog is unique to its manufacturer, but they all have certain items in common. The following items must be checked before you start printing your first job of the day:

- **Type of paper**. With inkjet printers, this setting is critical. Many users are disappointed with the photographs they print because the printer is set up to print to plain paper when photo paper is installed. Several newer printers automatically detect the type of paper that is installed.

- **Paper size**. Generally, it should be set to letter size in the United States.

- **Orientation**. Is the photo in landscape or portrait orientation? Does the setting of the printer match the orientation of what you are printing?

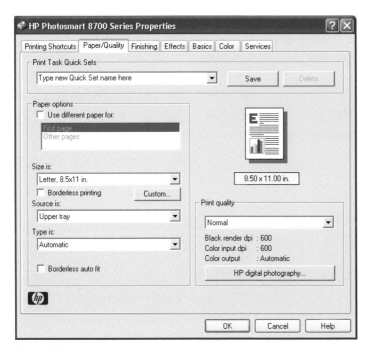

Figure 11.7
The dialog that appears for the printer properties is designed and provided by the printer manufacturer and, therefore, is unique.

Speeding Up Your Print Jobs

Printing a photo can take a lot of time. This section discusses some ways in which you can speed up the job while maintaining excellent results.

Flatten Your Picture

If you are about to print a photograph that contains layers, you can print out a photo quicker if you flatten the image before you print it. First, you need to save the photo as a PSD file to preserve the layers, but then save a copy and flatten the photo by using the Flatten Image command (found in the Layers menu).

Resolution—More Is Slower

Every printer manufacturer that sells printers that will be used for graphics or printing out photos heavily advertises the resolution of its printers. I am using an HP 8750 to proof my pages for this book. It advertises that it can print at a resolution of 4,800 dpi. That is an incredible resolution, so it stands to reason that a photo printed at that resolution would be razor sharp with fantastic detail, right? Actually, that's not true. The first stumbling block to this printing miracle is your eyes. That is more than most anyone's eyes can resolve. Ignoring that minor problem, when you print at the highest resolution that the printer can spit out, it consumes large amounts of ink and takes up to four times as long to print.

Getting the Best Quality Prints from Your Printer

The three most important things that affect the quality of the photographs that you print are the resolution settings, the paper quality, and the ink quality.

Working with PIM and Exif 2.2

Sometimes when you save an image you might get a message that tells you the PIM data isn't being preserved. So, just what is this, and do you need it? The acronym PIM stands for PRINT Image Matching and it is endorsed primarily by Epson and some other camera manufacturers. The idea behind this standard is that PIM-enabled digital cameras and printers are designed to share PIM data that allows them to produce the best possible prints.

Another attempt to digitally establish a common language for digital cameras and printers is the Exif 2.2, called Exif Print. Exif 2.2 uses the information (Exif tags) in photos from digital cameras that support Exif 2.2. The Exif Print-supported printer reads this information and, in theory, produces optimum quality photos. The advantage of Exif 2.2 is that it uses the existing Exif data format, which your digital camera already uses, whereas the PIM is proprietary.

Optimum Resolution Settings

So what resolution setting should you use to get the best possible photographic prints? For a majority of your printing, the default automatic photo setting should work great. If you go into one of the advanced settings pages (**Figure 11.8**), you might be surprised to discover that most photo printers don't even show the resolution setting used. This is because the printer companies heavily advertise the highest resolution capability of their printers and, therefore, users that are not familiar with resolution feel that they need to print at the highest resolution to get good quality prints. The truth is that normal photo print quality coming from a professional developer is far less than the highest possible resolution. The reason has to do with the human eye's limitation that we mentioned previously. If a photograph has a wide palette of colors, it's almost impossible to tell the difference between a photo printed at 720 dpi and one printed at 4,000 dpi.

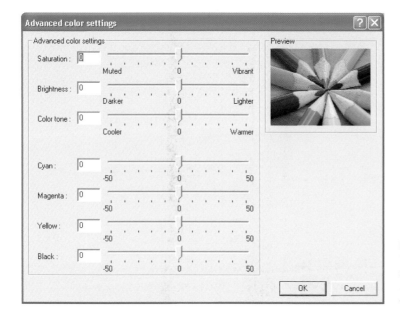

Figure 11.8
For all the advertising for monstrously high resolutions, most photo printers print beautifully at their photo default setting.

So when should you use the higher resolutions? If the photograph you are printing is 5 x 7 or larger, you might benefit from printing at a higher resolution. But don't take my word for it—run a little test and print your favorite photograph at the top three resolutions of your printer. See how long it takes to print each one and write on the back of each photo what resolution it was printed at. After you do that, put the photos in a file folder or a big manila envelope, and the next time you are tempted to print at a higher resolution, pull out those prints to remind yourself of the difference (or lack thereof).

Your Photo Is Only as Good as the Paper You Use

Like it or not, the best photo printer in the world produces pretty crummy photos when it prints them on copier paper. Another general fact of life: Your printer will do better on its own brand of specialty paper than it will with the generic stuff you bought at the local super center. This has nothing to do with the superiority of the printer manufacturer's paper and, even though I recommend their paper, I still have to buy my own just like you. It has to do with the settings of the printer software being fine-tuned to get the best-looking result using its own paper. Look at the list of papers (media) that are listed for my HP 8750 printer (see **Figure 11.9**). Two categories of paper are listed: A large variety of HP papers and others. Many of the HP printers automatically detect what type of paper is being used. Whether you have to select the paper in your printer manually or your printer detects it automatically, the important point is that the paper made by the manufacturer is matched to the printer and will produce the best results.

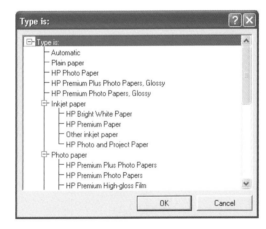

Figure 11.9
For the best possible photos from your printer, you should always use the specialty paper provided by the printer's manufacturer.

Now, if you are printing cute sticker buttons for your kid's birthday paper, making invites for a bash, or punching out the dreaded annual holiday newsletter, get the best deal on paper you can and go for it.

Ink Quality, Refills, and Other Fun Stuff

Because the cost of ink refills is getting to be almost as expensive as the printers, it becomes tempting to get generic ink cartridges or refill kits. I cannot address the non-photo ink refills because I haven't done any testing with them, but I have done some serious testing of the generic photo-printer inks, and they don't compare to the real thing. The colors are not the same; they are never as vivid as the original—period.

Anytime you notice that the colors of your inkjet printer aren't quite right, you need to run the test pattern and see if any of the printer's ink nozzles are blocked. If just one of the printhead nozzles are not working, a few of the colors in your photo can radically change. Clean the nozzles. This is especially true if you haven't printed on the printer in over a week. The printhead nozzles tend to dry up a bit.

Printing Multiple Copies of a Picture

One of the coolest features in Photoshop Elements is the capability to print many different-sized copies of a single image with a single click of a button. I'm talking about the Print Multiple Photos option.

You can activate the Print Multiple Photos feature by doing one of the following:

- Choose File, Print Multiple Pictures from the Editor.

- Choose File, Print from the Organizer.

- Click the Print Multiple Photos button in the Print Preview dialog.

Whichever method you choose, it launches the Print Photos dialog (**Figure 11.10**) in the Organizer.

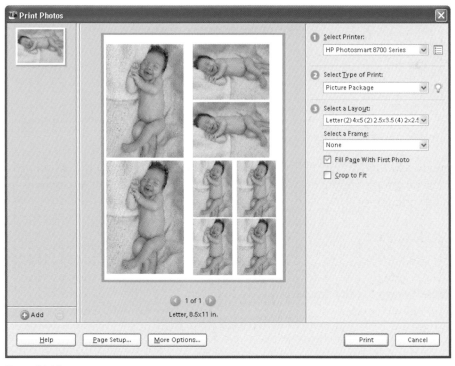

Figure 11.10
The Print Photos dialog.

Making a Contact Sheet

Contact sheets are invaluable summaries of the photos that you have. It's handy for referencing a number of photos at once. Here is how to make a contact sheet:

1. From Elements Editor choose File, Print Multiple Photos, opening the Print Photos dialog (**Figure 11.11**).

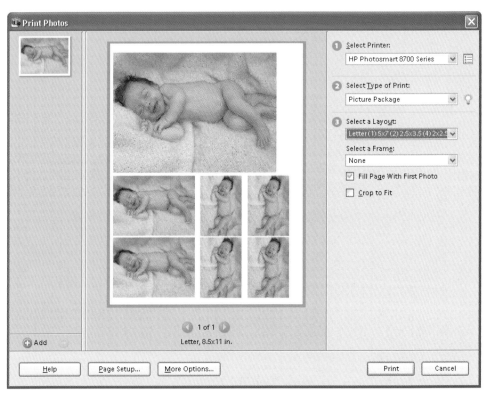

Figure 11.11
The Print Photos dialog is the starting point for multiple operations.

2. To select the photos to be included in the contact sheet, click the green Add icon in the lower-left corner of the dialog, which opens another dialog (**Figure 11.12**).

3. The choices for photo sources in this dialog is mind-boggling. Select the source from the Add Photos From section. Check the photos you want to include and then click the Add Selected Photos button. Click the OK button to return to the Print Photos dialog (**Figure 11.13**).

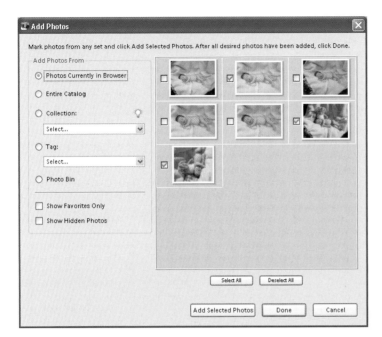

Figure 11.12
The Add Photos dialog, from which you select the photos to be included in the contact sheet.

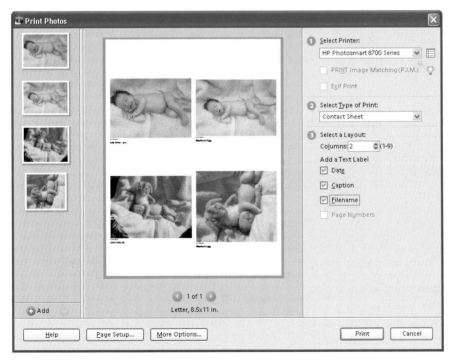

Figure 11.13
From here you can define how your contact sheet appears when it is created.

4. Check the Select Printer setting to ensure it is set to the correct printer. The icon is to the right of the printer selection in the Printer Properties box. Clicking on the icon opens the printer properties for the selected printer. Be aware that this part of the dialog will look different depending on the printer that you have installed.

5. Choose Contact Sheet from the Select Type of Print. Then choose the number of columns you want to use for the contact sheet.

6. Check what information you want included under the thumbnails when the contact sheet is printed. Once it's all selected, click the Print button. **Figure 11.14** shows a completed contact sheet.

TIP

As the number of columns increases, the size of the thumbnails on the contact sheet gets smaller and the number of pages (if there is more than one) decreases. Likewise, fewer columns mean bigger thumbnails and more total pages.

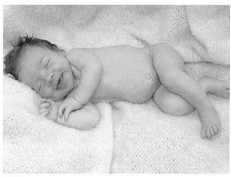

9/15/2004
baby before 1.psd

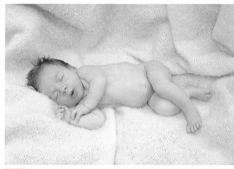

9/15/2004
libbyblanket2.jpg

9/15/2004
DSCN3442.JPG

9/15/2004
libbyblanket.jpg

Figure 11.14
The completed contact sheet.

Creating a Picture Package

Picture Package lets you create a limitless combination of photos and styles on a single page. For those of you who like to share prints of favorite photos with friends, the Picture Package allows you to place multiple copies of the same photo (or even different photos) all on the same page in much the same manner as the smaller sets of school photos are printed on single sheets of letter-sized photo paper.

Creating a Picture Package is done in nearly the same way as the previous contact sheets.

1. From the Organizer, choose File, Print, which opens the Print Photos dialog.

2. To select the photos to be included in the Picture Package (even if it is only one), click the Add icon in the lower-left corner of the dialog, which opens the Add Photos dialog.

3. Select the source containing the photo(s) you want to include in your Picture Package from the Add Photos From section. Check the photos you want to include, and then click the Add Selected Photos button. Then, click the OK button to return to the Print Selected Photos dialog.

4. Check Select Printer to ensure it is set to the correct printer. If you want to make a file rather than printing the image, make sure you choose Microsoft Office Imaging Document.

5. Select Picture Package from the Select Type of Print.

6. If you are making multiple copies of a single photo, make sure that you check the One Photo Per Page check box. Then, choose the layout you want to use and the preview reflects how it will appear when printed (**Figure 11.15**).

7. Wait—there's more. Adobe felt that you needed even more goodies on your Picture Package, so they added the option to add one of 24 frames like the one shown in **Figure 11.16**. Most of these jewels are too frilly for this Texan, but I am sure they will be appreciated by most users.

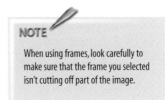

NOTE

When using frames, look carefully to make sure that the frame you selected isn't cutting off part of the image.

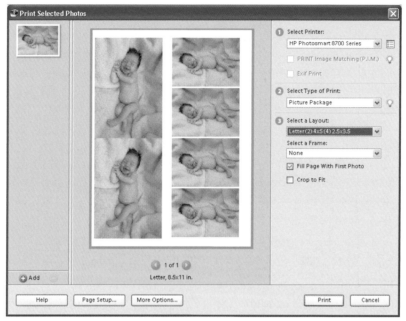

Figure 11.15
This represents only one of the more than 14 layout combinations.

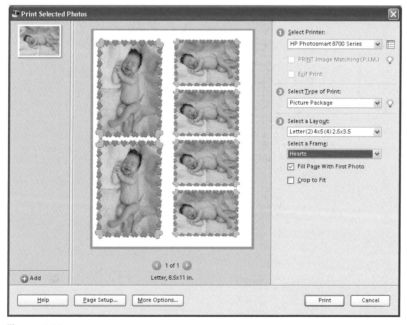

Figure 11.16
This is only one of the 24 different frames that are available to include with your Picture Package.

Getting Really Creative with Creations

Photoshop Elements lets you go far beyond just printing photos or attaching them to e-mails to send to friends. You can use your photos and video clips to create a great variety of photo albums, cards, postcards, wall calendars, Web photo galleries, and slide shows. The slide shows can be saved on CDs in a format called VCD, that lets them be played on a DVD player as well as another computer. Regardless of which one you make, they are all called creations.

If the idea of making something as complicated as a slide show or photo album makes your heart skip a beat, fear not. Most of the creations in Elements use a wizard that walks you through from start to finish. It is a step-by-step process in which you select one of the many templates, arrange your photos (hardest part), and when you are happy with it, you publish your creation.

Starting the Creation Process

From either the Editor or the Photo Browser in Organizer, you start the process by clicking the Create button ![Create] in the shortcut bar, opening the Creation Setup dialog (**Figure 11.17**). This is the jumping-off point—all creations begin here.

Figure 11.17
The Creation Setup dialog is the starting point for any creation that you want to make.

From here you select what you want to create in the left side of the dialog. As you select each item, a description of the creation appears in the lower-right corner of the dialog, as well as some tiny icons that indicate how the selected creation can be shared (**Figure 11.18**).

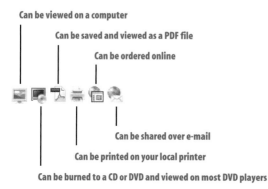

Figure 11.18
These icons tell you how the selected creation can be shared.

Create a Slide Show

Gone are the days when a slide show involved a slide projector and a box containing several hundred slides. Now you can easily make a slide show of your vacation, or an important event like a graduation or wedding. You can select the slides, organize them, add text and titles, and then save them in one of several formats to share with friends and loved ones. Here is how to make your very own slide show.

1. Before you begin, select the photos you want to include in your slide show in the photo browser by Ctrl-clicking each one you want to include (you can also select a sequence of photos by clicking on a thumbnail and Shift-selecting the last one in the sequence). From the Creation Setup dialog, select Slide Show and click the OK button in the lower-right corner.

2. Your first choice is to choose the preferences that you want to use for the slide show (**Figure 11.19**). After you have created several slide shows you will have a good idea about what features you generally want in all of your slide shows. Once you have the preferences set the way you want them, you can uncheck the Show this dialog option at the bottom so you won't have to see it every time you go to make a slide show.

3. When the Slide Show editor opens (**Figure 11.20**), the photos you selected in the Photo Browser appear across the bottom of the Editor. From here you can add text, graphics, music, narration, and select the type and duration of transitions.

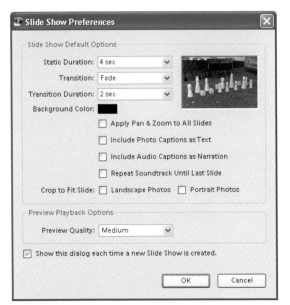

Figure 11.19
Select the preferences used in your slide shows.

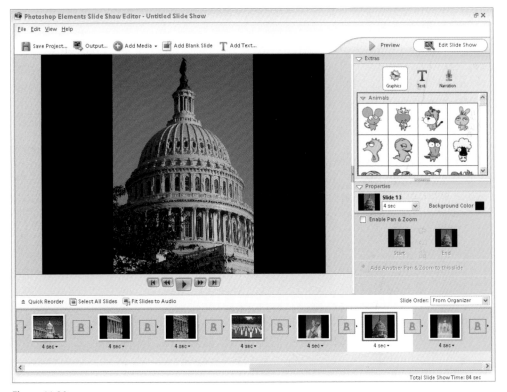

Figure 11.20
Select a folder containing photos that will be used in the slide show.

4. You can add additional photos to the slide show at any time by clicking the Add Media icon in the Slide Editor, then choosing the source for your photos when the Add Photos dialog opens. Select the photos you want to add by checking the boxes next to the thumbnails and click Done to return to the Slide Show Editor (**Figure 11.21**).

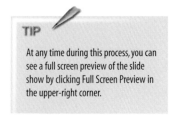

Figure 11.21
The slides are loaded and we're ready to make a slide show.

5. To add a title slide, click the Add Blank Slide. It appears to the right of the first slide. Click on the blank slide in the thumbnail row at the bottom and drag it to the far left to make it the first slide. You can rearrange any slide in the show this way. Click the Add Text button, and when the Add Text dialog opens add a title. I added the very original title: Our Trip to Washington, D.C. Feel free to use it. In the example shown (**Figure 11.22**), I also added some graphics, which included the background.

Figure 11.22
Add title page and a brilliant title.

6. Add some music (**Figure 11.23**, next page). Adobe has provided a nice collection of music to go with your slide shows. Click on the Add Media button. Choose Add Audio from Organizer and make your selection from the list of the recorded music that comes with Elements that appears. Pick something from the music selection, and then click OK. You can also load your own favorite music instead of using the music provided by Adobe by choosing Audio from Folder, and selecting the tune from a folder on your hard drive. Once the music is loaded, you can click Fit Slides to Audio, and the transition time of each slide will be set so that the slides fit the length of the selected music.

7. When you are finished with your slide show, you can save it in the Organizer (File, Save As). When the Slide Show Output dialog opens (**Figure 11.24**, next page), you can select the format for your slide show and give the slide show a name. The file that you save is in a unique format that can only be opened by the Slide Show Editor.

Figure 11.23
Adding music can really make your slide show special.

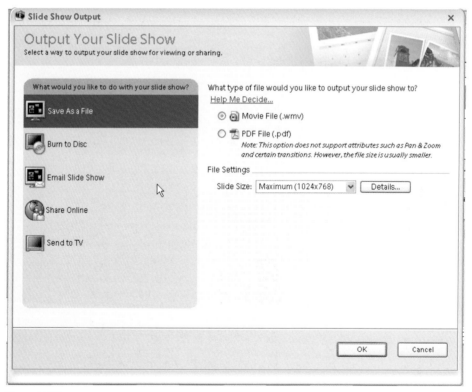

Figure 11.24
Saving the file in the Organizer.

8. To save your slide show in a format that can be shared with others, you must save it as a Windows Meta Video (WMV) file or burn it as a Video CD. You can select either one from the Slide Show Output dialog. The WMV files can be played by the Windows Media player and the Video CD can be played on most DVD players.

9. The second choice in the Creation list is VCD with Menu. This Creation allows you to put all of the slide shows that you made into a single Video CD with a menu.

Now that you know how to make a slide show, let's see what other creation is possible.

Create a Photo Album

With the Creation Setup wizard, you can lay out your favorite photos using a variety of templates and design styles, and then print a photo album using your photo printer.

1. From the Creation Setup dialog (see Figure 11.17), select Album Pages and click the OK button in the lower-right corner to start the wizard (**Figure 11.25**). The hardest part of using this wizard is that there's such a large number of choices that it is difficult to settle on one to use.

2. The next step is to add photos (**Figure 11.26**)

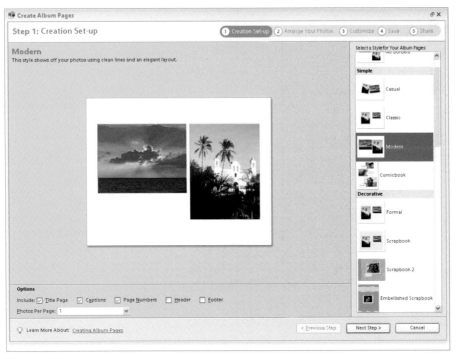

Figure 11.25
The Creation wizard for setting up the Album Pages.

Figure 11.26
Add and sort the photos you want in your Album Pages.

3. Now, if you like, add titles to the photos. The first photo is used as the title page. The photo's caption (if present) is replaced by the title text you add in this step. If you select Title but leave the title text blank, no text appears on the title page. A title page isn't mandatory, but a collection is improved by a brief descriptive title page (**Figure 11.27**).

4. To finish the project, save the Album Pages by giving them a name and choosing what format (PDF, e-mail or Print) you want to share your pages in. There are only two steps after customizing: Save and Share. Selecting Save, saves the album as a creation in Organizer. The Share step is optional, and you only have to use it if you want to export the album in a format others can look at. You can also go back and share an album from the shortcut menu in the Organizer.

The wizard for the Card, Postcard, and Wall Calendar is easy to use and so we won't cover it here. For details about these features, you can check the online user's guide or the user's manual.

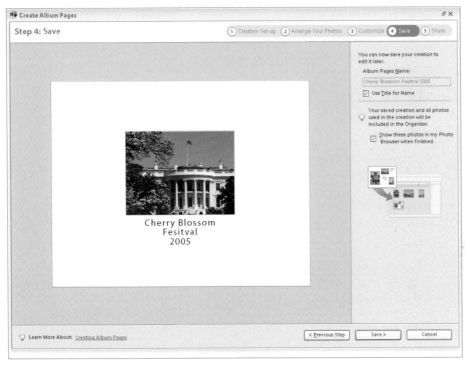

Figure 11.27
The addition of titles rounds out the photos on the pages.

Making an HTML Photo Gallery

Sending photos to people as e-mail is cool, but not nearly as cool as having your own Web page. If you are thinking, "I don't know the first thing about Web pages," then this next feature was made with you in mind. I have a confession to make at this point. I know next to nothing about Web pages myself, and yet I maintain a Web site with my latest photos (www.davehuss.com). So how do I do it? I use the HTML Photo Gallery in this program.

Here is a summary of how this works.

1. I pick the photos that I want to make into a Web page.

2. I select a template that seems appropriate for the photos from the HTML Photo Gallery Creation wizard. When finished, I have a set of files.

3. I copy the files to my Web site.

4. Anyone who accesses the Web site can then view the photos.

TIP

HTML Photo Gallery was called Web Photo Gallery in Photoshop Elements 3.

Getting A Web Site

So how do you get a Web site? If you have a cable modem, you often have Web space already available to you at no extra charge. In my case, I purchased the domain name davehuss.com and I also rent space on a Web hosting site. It doesn't cost much, I pay less than $40 per year for the whole thing. I still don't know anything about HTML or making Web pages, but with the help of HTML Photo Gallery I am able to maintain a Web page.

Running the HTML Photo Gallery

The HTML Photo Gallery wizard does everything necessary to create a Web photo gallery that, when loaded to a server, works as a Web site that features a home page with thumbnail images and gallery pages with full-size images.

1. Just as with a slide show, select the photos you want to include on your Web page by highlighting them in the Photo Browser before opening Creation Setup. From the Creation Setup select HTML Photo Gallery and click the OK button in the lower-right corner (**Figure 11.28**).

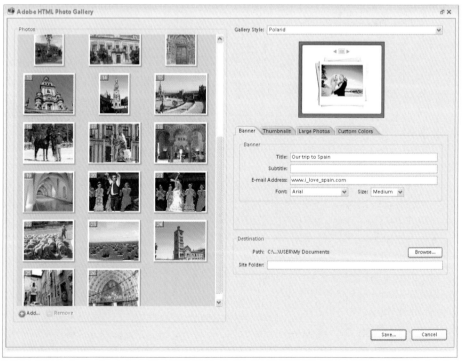

Figure 11.28
The HTML Photo Gallery wizard starts here.

2. As with the other Creation wizards, you add photos by clicking the Add icon and choosing the photos you want to appear in the Web page. This page can also be one of the most difficult. Adobe has included 38 Gallery Styles (**Figure 11.29**), making the choice of which one to use very difficult.

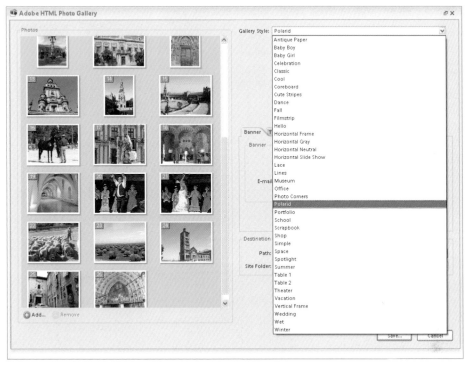

Figure 11.29
The next step involves the difficult decision of which gallery style to choose.

3. After adding your photos, you need to select the Banner tab and add Title, Subtitle, and so on (**Figure 11.30**, next page). You also need to add a destination for where the Web files made by HTML Photo Gallery will be stored. All of the other settings can be left at their default settings, if you want.

4. When you are finished, click Save, and the Web page will be built. When it is finished, the Web page you just created is launched (**Figure 11.31**, next page). The next step is to run the HTML Gallery again and make all the changes that you decide to make after you see the completed pages. Don't kid yourself, after you see the page, you'll start wondering what it would look like if you used a different font, thumbnail size, different gallery, and many other variables. Thus begins a long cycle of trying something different, rebuilding the Web page, and then trying another combination. There is just something that is addictive about it—in a fun way.

Figure 11.30
This is the title page of the finished Web page.

Figure 11.31
Here is one of the pages of the HTML Photo Gallery.

A Working with Raw Format

One of the exciting features of Photoshop Elements is the ability to import and work with Raw format images using the Camera Raw plug-in. While Raw is the image format of choice for professionals, many digital photographers either can't or don't use it. It was for this reason that I chose to make this section an appendix rather than a chapter in the mainstream of the book. If you aren't familiar with the Raw format, the first part of this appendix begins by explaining what the Raw format is, and the advantages of using it.

What Is Raw Format?

Many new mid-range to high-end digital cameras have the ability to save images in a unique format called Raw. The word Raw isn't an acronym, as you might think, but literally means raw, as in "unprocessed." It refers to a format containing the unprocessed data from the digital camera's sensor. The format name Raw is often written using all capital letters (RAW); but there is no standard for one way or another.

A Raw file contains the original image information, as it comes off the sensor before in-camera processing is applied. The Raw format is proprietary and differs from one manufacturer to another, and sometimes between cameras made by one manufacturer. The image must be processed and converted to an RGB format such as TIFF or JPEG before it can be manipulated using Photoshop Elements.

Can Elements Read Raw Files from My Camera?

Because new digital cameras are being introduced all the time, the ability to read and process Raw files from newer or improved models requires that the Camera Raw plug-in be frequently updated. If you go to www.adobe.com and search for Raw file support, you will find a list of the digital cameras that are currently supported. If your camera has a Raw format support but Elements doesn't support it, be patient. Continue to use the software provided by your manufacturer and keep checking the Adobe Web site for the next Camera Raw plug-in update.

All digital cameras can process the image from the sensor into a JPEG file using settings for white balance, color saturation, contrast, and sharpness that are either selected automatically or entered by the photographer before taking the picture. Cameras that support Raw files save these settings in the file for processing the image on your computer.

Does Your Camera Offer Raw Format?

The only way to tell if your camera offers Raw format is to read the manual. On every camera I have worked with, the choice of Raw format is part of the Quality settings. Quality settings are where you choose which JPEG setting to use, and they are selected either on the LCD menu or by clicking a button. The Raw format option is typically found on many mid-price to high-end consumer digital cameras and always on digital-SLR (Single Lens Reflex) cameras.

NOTE

In case you hadn't noticed the name, Camera Raw plug-in is a play on words. When you don't emphasize the ending "a" in camera, the name of the plug-in is Cam-er-Raw. Get it? While it's cute, it is generally accepted that if you have to explain the joke, it doesn't work.

How Regular and Raw Images Are Processed

A lot happens inside your digital camera from the moment you press the shutter button until the image is tucked away into your camera's media card. The digital data from the camera's image sensor is sent to the camera's internal processor, at which time the white balance (WB), exposure, and other settings are applied. Next, the image is converted from its raw 12 bits per channel format to a standard 8 bits per channel graphic format—typically JPEG, although some cameras can also save photos as TIFF files. Last, the processed files are stored on the media card (**Figure A.1**).

Figure A.1
Typical processing of a JPEG image.

If an image is saved using the Raw file format, the camera does not apply any processing of the sensor data except to include time/date, camera settings, and a lot of other data before saving it as a 12 bits per channel image (**Figure A.2**).

Figure A.2
Raw format does not process images in the camera.

When you open a Raw format file using Photoshop Elements, the program detects it as a Raw format file and opens the Camera Raw plug-in dialog (**Figure A.3**) to process the image, convert it, and open it in the workspace.

Figure A.3
The Camera Raw plug-in dialog.

Processing Choices

With Raw files, you do the processing on your computer with Photoshop Elements. When it comes to converting Raw files, you have several choices. The Camera Raw plug-in, a third-party conversion program such as Bibble (**Figure A.4**), or conversion software produced by the camera manufacturer (usually at additional cost) like the Nikon Capture (**Figure A.5**). Raw files have unique file extensions depending on who makes that camera. For example, a Raw format file from a Nikon camera has an NEF extension; Canon uses CRW; Olympus, ORF; Fuji, RAF; and Minolta MRW, to name only a few.

Figure A.4
Third-party software can be used to convert Raw files.

Figure A.5
Camera manufacturers also sell software to convert Raw files.

Why Use Raw?

Raw format files are often compared with film that has been exposed but not yet developed. The degree of control that is possible when opening a Raw format file is very impressive. Camera settings such as white balance, exposure, sharpening, and tone can be adjusted or changed when the image is opened. The image on the left in **Figure A.6** shows a Raw file that was opened with no changes applied to it while the image on the right had some adjustments made to it using the Camera Raw plug-in when it was opened.

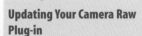

Updating Your Camera Raw Plug-in

It seems that every day some camera manufacturer offers a newer version of their digital cameras. Often the new camera produces a different version of Raw file and, as often is the case, Camera Raw does not recognize the Raw files produced by these newest cameras. To resolve this dilemma Adobe is continually updating the Camera Raw plug-in and makes the update available free on the Adobe website (www.adobe.com/support/downloads).

Figure A.6
Many color cast and exposure problems can be resolved using the Camera Raw plug-in feature of Elements. The image on the right has been corrected using the Camera Raw plug-in.

The only image problems that cannot be resolved using the Camera Raw plug-in controls are images that are out of focus and photos in which parts of the image have gone either completely white or black.

Another advantage to saving images as Raw files is that the image can be saved as a 16-bit/channel image. See the sidebar "Why 16-Bit Is Bigger than 24-Bit" for further details. Photoshop Elements offers limited support for 16-bit/channel images, but the features that are supported are the essential ones like Auto Levels, Auto Contrast, Shadows/Highlights, Levels, and many more. The advantage of saving an image as a 16-bit/channel is helpful for the following types of images:

- An image that needs to be resized (made larger).

- A prized photo that you want to make into a spectacular one.

- An image with limited tonal range to which either Auto Contrast or Auto Levels needs to be applied.

- A noisy image that requires some extensive work to clean up.

Resizing, correcting, or removing noise from a 16-bit/channel image will produce superior results than can be expected from applying the same actions to an 8-bit image. This is because a 16-bit/channel image has more color (tonal) information in it for Photoshop Elements to work with, and thus, you generally get superior results.

Why 16-Bit Is Bigger than 24-Bit

Referring to an image as 16-bit can be confusing. After all, the color depth of an image we typically work with is described as being 24-bit—therefore, describing an image as being 16-bit sounds like it would contain less color information, when it in fact has twice as much. The term 16-bit describes the number of bits per color channel, while 24-bit refers to the total number of bits in all three color channels. So a 16-bit image actually has a color depth of 48-bits (16 x 3 color channels). So why not call them 48-bit images? Therein lies a mystery. Several years ago, scanners began offering the ability to send unprocessed (raw) data to the computer in 16-bit-per-channel format. They described the files as having a color depth of 48-bit. When digital cameras began to offer the same ability, the images were described as being 16-bit (per channel). For reasons unknown to this cowboy, the 16-bit handle stuck and continues to gain in popularity.

Disadvantages of Raw

Along with all the advantages of the Raw format come some drawbacks. It takes much longer to open Raw files and process them than it does with JPEGs, due to their larger size. Workflow is another factor when working with Raw files. While a JPEG image can be attached to an e-mail or viewed by almost any Windows or Mac application, a Raw format file must be converted before it can be used with any application.

As noted above, Raw files are larger than JPEGs. For example, a 512 MB CompactFlash (CF) card on my camera can hold either 51 Raw images or 179 images if saved as high-quality JPEG images. With the cost of memory cards decreasing every day, that shouldn't be a major concern, but it is still a factor when going out to take photos. It should also be noted that using Raw on cameras that are not digital SLRs can increase the time between shots because the larger file takes longer to write to the memory card. This is why professional digital cameras have large buffers that allow photographers to continue to take more photos while the previous images are still being written to the memory card.

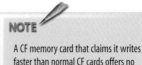

NOTE

A CF memory card that claims it writes faster than normal CF cards offers no advantage on cameras that are not digital SLRs. This is because the write-accelerated memory usually operates from five to ten times faster than the non-SLR camera can write.

The Camera Raw Plug-in Dialog

Before working with a Raw file, here is a quick look at the essential parts of the Camera Raw plug-in dialog (**Figure A.7**).

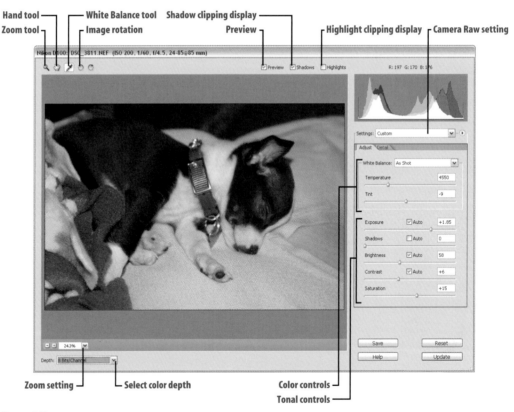

Figure A.7
The Camera Raw plug-in dialog.

The controls for the Camera Raw plug-in are organized by their functions. Some of them are self-explanatory while others could use some explanation.

In the upper-left corner are the standard Zoom and Hand tools, while the tool next to these two standard icons (the one that looks like the Eyedropper tool) is the White Balance tool. The color and tonal control give you an enormous amount of control over the color temperature, contrast, and other aspects of the image when the Raw file is processed. The two icons next to White Balance are for quick 90 degree rotation either left or right. For more information, see the sidebar "What Is Color Temperature and White Balance?"

When either the Shadows or Highlights check box at the top of the dialog is enabled, the preview window shows areas of the image that have turned pure black (shadow) or pure white (highlight).

The Settings area is where you can save your current settings in order to apply them to other Raw files when you open them. The controls are divided into two areas by the Adjust and Detail tabs. In most situations you will only be using the Adjust tab because the three sliders in the Details tab (Sharpness, Luminance Smoothing, and Color Noise Reduction) are more advanced settings that are best left at their default settings. In the next section, we'll open and process a Raw file, as well as learn how to use it.

What Is Color Temperature and White Balance?

These are terms that you hear a lot when working with digital cameras. Quite simply, color temperature is a measure of the color produced by light. You know that on a bright, sunny day, subjects tend to have a bluish color cast, and yet, as the sun begins to set, everything appears to take on an orange tint. The color temperature ranges from cool colors to warm colors and is measured in degrees Kelvin. Ironically, the higher the color temperature, the cooler the colors produced—the opposite of what we would expect.

White balance (WB) is a setting that establishes neutral colors, which is the key to accurate color reproduction. In camera film, the chemical composition of the film determines what colors are produced when it is properly exposed. Most film that people use to shoot pictures is balanced for daylight. A digital camera doesn't have a preset balance and must try to automatically calculate the correct WB (called automatic white balance, or AWB). While cameras are improving all of the time, oftentimes the digital camera gets fooled, and the result is an unwanted color cast, which should be removed using either the Camera Raw plug-in or the Editor in Photoshop Elements. When you open a Raw image, Elements attempts to read the WB setting that was included in the Raw file by the camera. If the WB setting in the dialog is set to As Shot, it uses the camera's white balance settings that are part of the image. Elements can't read the white balance settings with some digital cameras, either because the camera is a new model or the manufacturer used a non-standard format for the WB information. In such cases, Elements reads the image data and automatically calculates the white balance the best it can.

An Exercise in Processing Raw Files in Elements

If you are new to working with Raw files, you may feel that there are so many adjustments that you don't know where to begin. I recommend the following order of events:

- Rotate—if required.

- White balance correction.

- Adjust exposure.

- Tweak shadow and contrast.

- Other adjustments—only as needed.

To really get a feel for the power of working with Raw files, I have provided a Raw file to use for this exercise. **Puppy.nef** (NEF is the extension for a Nikon Raw file) is available for download on the Peachpit Press Web site. Because of the large size of the Raw format, the files are compressed and must first be uncompressed before you can use them.

1. With Elements in the Standard Edit mode, open the file **Puppy.nef**. Photoshop Elements automatically detects that this is a Raw file and opens the Camera Raw plug-in dialog (**Figure A.8**). By default, the Auto check boxes are selected when the Camera Raw dialog opens.

2. Change the White Balance to Auto. This creates a bluish cast to the image. Correct the white balance by selecting the White Balance tool and then click on the white fur of the dog. Notice how the Temperature slider changes each time you click on a different white area of the dog's fur (**Figure A.9**). With the white balance corrected, the image remains slightly blue because the light of the flash makes colors appear cooler. See the sidebar "Accurate Vs. Desired Color" for more details. If you want a warmer image, choose the Flash preset in the White Balance menu.

NOTE

Adjustments to a photo made by controls using the Auto setting aren't necessarily the best settings. This is because Elements can't make decisions based on seeing the photo as a picture, but rather by making changes based strictly on its analysis of pixel values.

TIP

You can change the default settings that are applied when the Camera Raw dialog is opened by changing the settings to what you want and then from the Settings menu choose Set Camera Default.

TIP

If there are no neutral colors in the image to select for Automatic White Balance, you can adjust the White Balance setting manually using either one of the White Balance presets or dragging the Temperature and Tint sliders.

Figure A.8
Auto White Balance corrects color temperature.

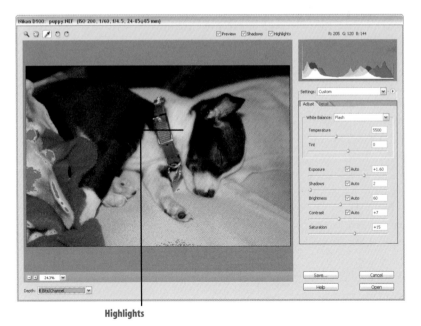

Highlights

Figure A.9
Areas that have become pure white are indicated in the preview.

3. Before making any adjustments to exposure, click the Shadows and Highlights buttons at the bottom of the screen. Areas of the image that are too bright (blowouts) appear as red. Areas that are too dark appear blue in the preview. In this case it is only a tiny reflection in the blanket and the puppy's collar, which are not critical. Had there been large areas of either red or blue, you could adjust the Exposure slider until the highlighted areas disappear. See the sidebar "What's Too Dark or Too Light?" for more details.

4. At this point you have made the most important corrections. If your photo seems a little flat, try adjusting the Shadows slider. There are many more controls that can be adjusted. If you will be working on the image using Elements, you shouldn't apply noise reduction or sharpening in the Camera Raw plug-in dialog.

Saving Your Raw Photos

Once you are satisfied with the color and tonal correction, you have several options when it comes to saving the images. Here are some basic facts about saving images from the Camera Raw plug-in:

- When the file is opened, the file extension and bits-per-channel information are displayed in the title bar (**Figure A.10**).

- You cannot save the files in the original Raw format you started with.

What's Too Dark or Too Light?

While it is great to use the Shadows and Highlights feature to visibly see areas in the photo that are either too white or too dark, you should be aware that it isn't necessary to adjust the exposure to prevent both of them. This is because the program can't tell the difference between part of the image that is blown out (gone to pure white) and contains detail that must be preserved and blowouts that are acceptable. For example, there are occasions when there will be small areas of pure white (like the reflection of a light in someone's glasses) or solid black (like dark areas of the dog's black fur) when the exposure is properly adjusted.

Accurate Vs. Desired Color

A question that often arises when you are correcting colors in an image is, should you make the colors accurate or make them look as you want them to look? Most ad agencies, for example need to be concerned with accurate colors. I encourage you to make the colors look like you want them to appear. For example, in the exercise with the puppy on the blanket the goal isn't to make the colors as they were at the moment the flash fired, but to make them appear warmer so the photo has even more appeal to the viewer.

- Changes that you make when opening a Raw file aren't applied as permanent changes to the Raw file; instead, changes are maintained in a separate file and can be applied when the file is opened at a later time. This maintains the integrity of the original Raw file.

- You can save images as either 8 bits per channel or 16 bits per channel. Saving as a 16-bit/channel image creates much larger files with increased color information, but eventually you will need to convert them to 8 bits per channel to use the image in most applications. In most cases, you should save images as 8 bits per channel.

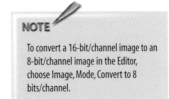

NOTE

To convert a 16-bit/channel image to an 8-bit/channel image in the Editor, choose Image, Mode, Convert to 8 bits/channel.

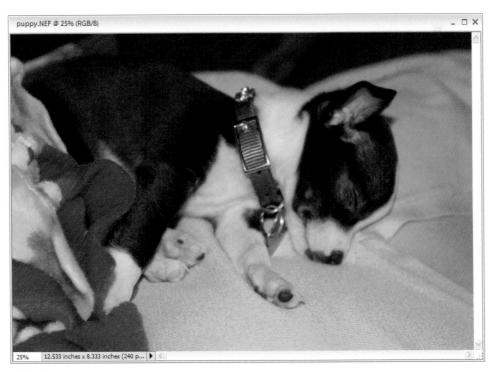

Figure A.10
The type and channel bit depth are displayed when the file is opened.

Adobe Digital Negative

Adobe has defined a new file format for handling Raw format files. It is called the Digital Negative specification and it describes a uniform way of storing the Raw data created by any digital camera. The specification offers something that is currently missing from the Raw format—a common standard. Similar to existing camera-specific Raw formats, a Digital Negative (DNG) is composed of two parts: the actual image data and the metadata that describes it. The format of the image data is very similar to the existing format used by digital cameras today. The key to the power of the Digital Negative format is in its metadata, which contains all the information needed to convert the Raw file into a standard graphics format.

There are many ways in which you might see the Digital Negative manifest in your digital photography experience. In the future, digital cameras will begin to support the format directly, either as their default Raw format or as an optional choice. Alternatively, manufacturers may include conversion utilities to convert their proprietary Raw formats into a Digital Negative file. But both of those are future events—what can you do now?

Also available from Adobe is the Digital Negative Converter, which converts the Raw format from more than 60 different digital cameras, the same cameras supported by the current Adobe Camera Raw plug-in found in both Photoshop and Photoshop Elements—into DNG files. This converter is available at no charge from the Adobe Web site. It allows you to take advantage of the archival benefits of Digital Negatives or to convert your camera-specific Raw files for use in a Raw converter that supports Digital Negatives. Additionally, the current Adobe Camera Raw plug-in of Elements is already Digital Negative-compatible. By converting your camera-specific Raw files to Digital Negatives, you can archive your Raw images without fear that at some later date your camera manufacturer's conversion software will no longer recognize its older Raw format (which has happened already). By archiving your Raw images to a DNG format you will always be able to open and use them a few years or a few decades from now.

B Using Pressure-Sensitive Tablets

One of the greatest tools you can buy to improve your work with Photoshop Elements is a pressure-sensitive tablet. These tablets (also called digitizing or digitizer tablets, or Wacom tablets), provide you with an input device that is in the shape of a pen. If you have never worked with a pressure-sensitive tablet, you will be surprised how easy it is to work on images with a pen rather than a mouse.

Not only is the shape of the stylus (the pen) something we are accustomed to, but the digitizer tablet is an absolute pointing device in comparison to a mouse (which is a relative positioning device). See the sidebar, "Relative Vs. Absolute Positioning" for more information. To demonstrate the difference, in **Figure B.1** I signed my name with a mouse and with my Wacom tablet. You should be able to tell which is which without me even telling you. (OK, the red was written with the mouse.)

Figure B.1
Which one was written with a pressure-sensitive pen and which with a mouse?

My first experience with a digitizer pad (yet another name for the tablet) was over ten years ago. They were large, very expensive, and had more than their share of software conflicts with other applications. There were quite a few tablet vendors back then, but few would disagree that today Wacom has become the industry standard in this area. Recently, I have seen some new vendors offering pressure-sensitive tablets, and while I haven't tried them all, I have yet to use a tablet with better feel and operation than my Wacom.

NOTE

During a conference, I was approached by a person after my workshop who declared that he could write with a mouse very well. I told him he needed to date more.

In the early days of pressure-sensitive tablets, purchasing one could cost several thousand dollars. Today, I have seen Wacom's Graphire tablets selling for under $100. **Figure B.2** is a photo of the Graphire Bluetooth tablet that I use with my laptop computer. What makes this tablet even cooler than the previous tablets I've used is that it is completely wireless. No cord on the pen and no cord between the tablet and the computer.

Relative Vs. Absolute Positioning

A mouse is a relative positioning device. That means that as you move the mouse, it sends information to the computer about how far in any particular direction it is being moved. If there is an obstacle on the desk, you simply pick up the mouse, move it back toward you, and move it again. The cursor on the screen is unaware that the actual position of the mouse was changed when you picked it up and moved it.

An absolute positioning device, like a digitizer tablet, tells the computer where on the digitizer pad that the pen is located. To move the screen cursor from the left to the right side of the screen requires that you move the stylus from the left to the right side of the pad.

If you have used a mouse for any amount of time, you will be surprised how accustomed you have become to relative positioning. Wacom recommends using only the pen for everything for the first three days you use the tablet (put the mouse away). After three days, you will be able to use the pen and mouse equally well. And some users report that their tablet alleviates their mouse and trackball-induced repetitive stress injuries.

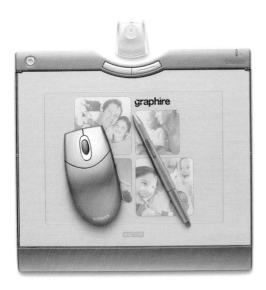

Figure B.2
The Graphire Bluetooth pressure-sensitive tablet is an excellent choice for working with Photoshop Elements.

What Does Pressure-Sensitive Mean?

Pressure-sensitive means that when you press the stylus on the pad, it literally detects the full range of pressure from the pen on the tablet. When used with a pressure-sensitive tool, such as Photoshop Elements' Clone Stamp tool, Liquify Filter, or the Brush tool, you discover a new dimension of control. Press hard, and the parameters of the tool change. In some exercises in the other chapters of this book, I have had the reader stop to change a brush size or opacity setting before proceeding. With a pressure-sensitive brush, these parameters can be changed by increasing or decreasing the pressure on the tablet surface. It feels more natural because that's how brushes work in the real world.

NOTE

While using pressure information to control tools in Elements is important, the truth is that even if they weren't pressure-sensitive, the feel of the pen and absolute positioning are a tremendous help when retouching or making selections.

Dave's Favorite Tablet Questions

When I teach a workshop, I typically get questions from users who have never owned a tablet before. Here are my favorites because they're good questions:

- **If I use a tablet, will I have to give up my mouse?** No. In the early days of tablets, this was an issue, but today your mouse and your tablet can both be active at the same time.

- **Since the tablet ships with a mouse, do I have to use it?** No. Even though a fine mouse was included with my Graphire tablet. I prefer my favorite wireless optical mouse.

- **Will the tablet work with all of Elements tools?** Yes and no. Yes, it works with everything in Elements. Not all of the Elements tools use the pressure information. For example, what affect would you expect increasing pressure would do to the Type tool?

- **Does the pressure-sensitive tablet work with other software applications, or does it only work with Elements?** All software applications can receive positioning information from a tablet, and many applications can use pressure-sensitive input from a digitizer tablet.

- **Will it work on my Mac?** Yes, it works great under OS X.

- **Does the pen use batteries?** No, it gets its power from the cosmic energy of the universe (kidding). The pen and mouse from Wacom are cordless and battery-free. They are powered by radio signals from the tablet. Wacom calls this "electromagnetic resonance." The USB version of the tablet draws its power through the USB connection to the attached computer. The Bluetooth tablet uses a rechargeable, lithium battery.

Using Elements with Your Pressure-Sensitive Pen

To get the most out of your pressure-sensitive tablet, you need to tell Elements how you want a particular tool to respond when you press either hard or soft. One of the greatest improvements of Elements with regards to its operation with pressure-sensitive pens is how Adobe has streamlined the settings. Bravo, Adobe.

Many programs that support pressure-sensitive tablets offer a daunting list of tool parameters that are changed based on the pressure information that is received. It is often so complicated that few ever use it. An example of Element's simplified approach is the Tablet options for the Brush tools (**Figure B.3**). They are basic and, more importantly, essential for retouching and making selections.

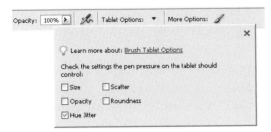

Figure B.3
The tablet controls for the Brush tools in Elements.

In addition to the tablet support for the individual tools, you can customize your pressure-sensitive tablet using the software control panel provided by your tablet manufacturer (**Figure B.4**).

From this panel you can customize stylus button settings, control how the stylus acts (like a mouse or a pen), define what part of the tablet is active (important with large tablets), vary brush tool properties, and much, much more.

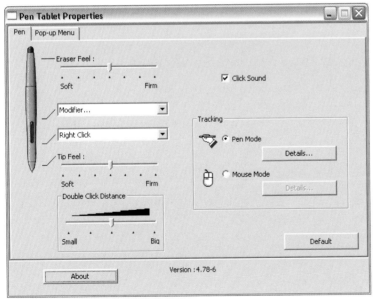

Figure B.4
This control panel for the Wacom Graphire is representative of some of the many features that can be customized.

Index